T0219848

Introducing
Materialize

Anirudh Prabhu
Aravind Shenoy

Apress®

Introducing Materialize

Anirudh Prabhu
Mumbai, India

Aravind Shenoy
Mumbai, Maharashtra, India

ISBN-13 (pbk): 978-1-4842-2348-2
DOI 10.1007/978-1-4842-2349-9

ISBN-13 (electronic): 978-1-4842-2349-9

Library of Congress Control Number: 2016961298

Copyright © 2016 by Anirudh Prabhu and Aravind Shenoy

This work is subject to copyright. All rights are reserved by the Publisher, whether the whole or part of the material is concerned, specifically the rights of translation, reprinting, reuse of illustrations, recitation, broadcasting, reproduction on microfilms or in any other physical way, and transmission or information storage and retrieval, electronic adaptation, computer software, or by similar or dissimilar methodology now known or hereafter developed.

Trademarked names, logos, and images may appear in this book. Rather than use a trademark symbol with every occurrence of a trademarked name, logo, or image we use the names, logos, and images only in an editorial fashion and to the benefit of the trademark owner, with no intention of infringement of the trademark.

The use in this publication of trade names, trademarks, service marks, and similar terms, even if they are not identified as such, is not to be taken as an expression of opinion as to whether or not they are subject to proprietary rights.

While the advice and information in this book are believed to be true and accurate at the date of publication, neither the authors nor the editors nor the publisher can accept any legal responsibility for any errors or omissions that may be made. The publisher makes no warranty, express or implied, with respect to the material contained herein.

Managing Director: Welmoed Spahr
Acquisitions Editor: Louise Corrigan
Technical Reviewer: Phil Nash
Editorial Board: Steve Anglin, Pramila Balan, Laura Berendson, Aaron Black, Louise Corrigan, Jonathan Gennick, Todd Green, Robert Hutchinson, Celestin Suresh John, Nikhil Karkal, James Markham, Susan McDermott, Matthew Moodie, Natalie Pao, Gwenan Spearing
Coordinating Editor: Nancy Chen
Copy Editor: Mary Behr
Compositor: SPi Global
Indexer: SPi Global
Artist: SPi Global, cover image courtesy of Freepik

Distributed to the book trade worldwide by Springer Science+Business Media New York, 233 Spring Street, 6th Floor, New York, NY 10013. Phone 1-800-SPRINGER, fax (201) 348-4505, e-mail orders-ny@springer-sbm.com, or visit www.springer.com. Apress Media, LLC is a California LLC and the sole member (owner) is Springer Science + Business Media Finance Inc (SSBM Finance Inc). SSBM Finance Inc is a Delaware corporation.

For information on translations, please e-mail rights@apress.com, or visit www.apress.com.

Apress and friends of ED books may be purchased in bulk for academic, corporate, or promotional use. eBook versions and licenses are also available for most titles. For more information, reference our Special Bulk Sales–eBook Licensing web page at www.apress.com/bulk-sales.

Any source code or other supplementary materials referenced by the author in this text are available to readers at www.apress.com. For detailed information about how to locate your book's source code, go to www.apress.com/source-code/. Readers can also access source code at SpringerLink in the Supplementary Material section for each chapter.

Printed on acid-free paper

I dedicate this to my mother and father for their endless support and words of encouragement. I also dedicate this to my many friends who have supported me throughout the process. I will always appreciate all they have done.

—Anirudh Prabhu

Contents at a Glance

Contents

About the Authors

Anirudh Prabhu is a UI Developer with more than seven years of experience. He specializes in HTML, CSS, JavaScript, jQuery, Sass, LESS, Twitter, and Bootstrap. Additionally, he has been associated with Packt and Apress books as a Tech Reviewer for several titles. He is the author of *Beginning CSS Preprocessors: With Sass, Compass, and Less* (Apress, 2015).

He has exposure to CoffeeScript and AngularJS. He's also been involved in building training material for HTML, CSS, and jQuery for twenty19 (`www.twenty19.com`), which is a portal for providing training for freshers/interns. In his free time, he enjoys listening to music and is also an avid photographer who likes taking unique photos.

Aravind Shenoy A senior technical writer by profession, Aravind's core interests are technical writing, content writing, content development, web design, and business analysis. Born and raised in Mumbai, he still resides there. A music buff, he loves listening to rock n' roll and rap. An engineering graduate from the Manipal Institute of Technology and an author of several books, he is a keen learner and believes that there is a steep learning curve, as Life is all about learning. In summary, as he quips, "The most important thing is to be happy."

About the Technical Reviewer

Phil Nash is a developer evangelist for Twilio, serving developer communities in London and all over the world. He is a Ruby, JavaScript, and Swift developer, a Google Developer Expert, a blogger, a speaker, and occasionally a brewer. He can be found hanging out at meetups and conferences, playing with new technologies and APIs, or writing open source code.

Acknowledgments

I dedicate this book to my aunt Godavari, my uncle Satish Rao, my cousin Ashwin, and finally my niece Ajnya, who is the light of my life. I miss her a lot. She taught me to take it easy and to understand the Leonard Cohen quote "There is a crack in everything. That's how the light gets in." I would also like to thank the entire Apress team (and Springer) and the Reviewer for the effort and time they put into this book. I sincerely appreciate it! This is my ninth book, but this time as a co-author, so I would like to thank the main author, Anirudh, who had to tolerate my idiosyncrasies. Finally, as Carrie Hope said, "Happiness is always there. You just have to choose to see it. There's no point dwelling in the dark and ignoring the light of the stars." Thanks to everyone. I really appreciate it.

—Aravind Shenoy

CHAPTER 1

■ ■ ■

Introducing Materialize

Materialize is an intuitive framework along the lines of Bootstrap and Foundation. It adheres to the Material Design language launched by Google. Materialize has UI components baked in, which are easy to use and implement, and it provides styling and animations for constructing aesthetic and responsive web sites. It takes into consideration several aspects such as browser portability and responsiveness, all within a compact footprint.

This chapter is a quick start guide to help you get to a grip on the concept of Material Design and an overview of Materialize and how it fits in the paradigm of Material Design.

In this chapter, I will be discussing the following topics:

- What is Material Design?

- What is Materialize CSS?

- Downloading Materialize

- Setting up Materialize

- Third party add-ons

- Sass parts

- A showcase of websites

What Is Material Design?

Material Design, created by Google, is a design philosophy that is inspired by real materials and helps create sleek and interactive web sites. It follows the Google's device-agnostic paradigm and stresses the need for web sites to look the same irrespective of the platform; in other words, uniformity across all devices, such as a tablet or phone or laptop.

Material design competes with other innovative competition such as flat design and metro design. However, it is a distinct concept that helps create a consistent and unified experience that gives a real-world look and is aesthetically pleasing.

Electronic supplementary material The online version of this chapter (doi:10.1007/978-1-4842-2349-9_1) contains supplementary material, which is available to authorized users.

Material Is Analogy

Material Design and development is inspired by understanding tactile elements used in the real world. This innovative concept is grounded in reality and is actually influenced by paper and ink. It draws and extends from the real world in a selective way, meaning it takes into account only those elements that will result in an awesome user experience. In short, it tries to incorporate the way actual materials in the world look and behave, meaning it doesn't treat your device as a two-dimensional platform. It results in a uniform and visually appealing experience for the users.

Bold, Graphic, Intentional

Typography, space, imagery, and scale are prime when it comes to print media design. Material design is not focused on creating just a visually appealing web site; rather it provides meaning as well and enhances the focus, resulting in an immersive user experience wherein the character or functionality becomes clear and explicitly.

Motion Provides Meaning

This paradigm is focused on ensuring that motion should be meaningful and appropriate. Animation is key to Material Design, which stresses that the transition is effective and coherent and not for the sake of it. It should work meaningfully and naturally, where you can perceive the way an object moves akin to a real-world situation. The physicality of the real world movement must be retained to create a seamless user experience. More information on Material Design methodology can be found on Google's Material Design site at https://material.google.com/.

What Is Materialize CSS?

 Materialize is an intuitive framework similar to Bootstrap and Foundation that offers ample UI components. However, the function differs because Bootstrap and Foundation are based on the mobile-first approach whereas Materialize adheres to Google's Material Design philosophy.

Downloading Materialize CSS

Materialize is available in two variants: production-ready and Sass (Figure 1-1).

Materialize

This is the standard version that comes with both the minified and unminified CSS and JavaScript files. This option requires little to no setup. Use this if you are unfamiliar with Sass.

Sass

This version contains the source SCSS files. By choosing this version you have more control over which components to include. You will need a Sass compiler if you choose this option.

Figure 1-1. *Materialize CSS and Sass versions*

Production-Ready

The production-ready version is a no-frills one that includes minified as well as un-minified CSS and JavaScript files. This version requires hardly any setup and can be included in your document. It doesn't include Sass and is for those users who are looking to use the framework and don't need to build and compile Sass code.

Sass Version

This version contains the SCSS files that are finally compiled to the final CSS files. Using this method, you can gain more control and decide which components to use. You can also customize the components as per the requirement. However, you need a Sass compiler if you use this method.

You can use any variant as per your requirement.

While the previous options (Materialize and Sass versions) required you to download, extract, and then include them in your web site directory, there is an alternative in which you can incorporate Materialize without any download. Here you do not need to download the Materialize locally. All you need to do is incorporate Materialize in your HTML file using a CDN (Content Delivery Network).

There are several advantages of using a CDN:

- It removes the load on your server by serving these scripts and assets from fast CDN servers that are available across the globe, dedicated for this task.

- CDN servers have high availability.

- Since the scripts files are on a CDN, which is a different server, you can achieve concurrency

- It offers enhanced control over asset delivery.

■ **Note** Using CDN requires an internet connection for the implementation to take place.

You can find the CDN at `https://cdnjs.com/libraries/materialize`. You can use Materialize in your design by including the specific link in your HTML document, as depicted in Listing 1-1.

Listing 1-1. Including Materialize Through CDN

```
<link rel="stylesheet" href="https://cdnjs.cloudflare.com/ajax/libs/
materialize/0.97.7/css/materialize.min.css">
<script src="https://cdnjs.cloudflare.com/ajax/libs/materialize/0.97.7/js/
materialize.min.js"></script>
```

Alternative Downloading Methods

The latest release of Materialize is available for Node.js and can be installed by using the NPM (Node Package Manager). The Node package comes with the source as well as the compiled CSS and JavaScript files. This package contains both source and compiled variants of CSS and JavaScript files. You can install Materialize using Node via the command prompt using the code in Listing 1-2.

Listing 1-2. Using Materialize via npm

```
npm install materialize-css
```

Alternatively, Materialize is also available with Bower, which too contains both the source files along with the compiled CSS and JavaScript files. Listing 1-3 contains the code to install Materialize using the Bower package from the command prompt.

Listing 1-3. Using Materialize via Bower

```
bower install materialize
```

Apart from Node and Bower, there are third party add-ons such as Ruby Gem, Meteor Package, and Ember packages that can be used to install Materialize.

Setting Up Materialize

Download the production-ready source files into the directory that houses the web site files. Extracting the files in your project directory after downloading will look as depicted in Figure 1-2.

Figure 1-2. *Directory structure after extracting Materialize*

The extracted folder contains folder for `css` to hold the CSS files, a `js` folder to hold the js files, a `fonts` folder to hold a local copy of roboto and the material icon font. Note that the directory structure contains the minified and un-minified versions. The min file means that all the whitespaces and extra characters have been removed or commented. It reduces the size of the file significantly, thereby increasing the speed resulting in better performance. The minified version is used for production environment whereas the un-minified version is used during development as it is more readable and suitable for debugging.

Materialize's JavaScript components are created using jQuery, so you also need to include jQuery library in your code when you plan to use its JavaScript.

Listing 1-4 contains a simple HTML file with Materialize's basic markup.

Listing 1-4. Code in index.html

```
<!DOCTYPE html>
  <html>
    <head>
      <!--Import Google Icon Font-->
      <link href="http://fonts.googleapis.com/icon?family=Material+Icons"
rel="stylesheet"/>
      <!--Import materialize.css-->
      <link type="text/css" rel="stylesheet" href="css/materialize.min.css"
media="screen,projection"/>

      <!--Let browser know website is optimized for mobile-->
      <meta name="viewport" content="width=device-width,
initial-scale=1.0"/>
    </head>
```

```
<body>
  <!--Import jQuery before materialize.js-->
  <script type="text/javascript" src="https://code.jquery.com/jquery-
  2.1.1.min.js"></script>
  <script type="text/javascript" src="js/materialize.min.js"></script>
</body>
</html>
```

■ **Note**   Including scripts at the bottom ensures that the actual page content is loaded first; when the scripts are finally downloaded, the content (DOM) will be ready for your scripts to manipulate.

■ **Note**   In any web design project, apart from the framework files, when you create the index.html file, you also create a separate style.css file because presentation (styling) should be kept separate from markup (HTML). It helps in easy organization and maintenance and should be located preferably in the css file folder. Another important aspect is the creation of the images folder, which you need to keep your images separate for better upkeep and accessibility without clubbing everything together in one file.

SASS Setup

Sass extends the capabilities of CSS with features and constructs that are not available in normal CSS. It is surely a way to write more maintainable code. With mixins, functions, and variables, you can customize material components faster than using vanilla CSS. As the web pages get more complex, stylesheets get larger and harder to maintain. Sass allows you to modularize your code and improves the workflow significantly.

Finally, if you are using a Sass version of Materialize, you need to deviate from the no-frills method explained in the preceding paragraphs. The extracted directory contains many .scss (basically Sass) files, which bring a new dimension to your web designing projects. The directory structure will be different and is shown in Figure 1-3.

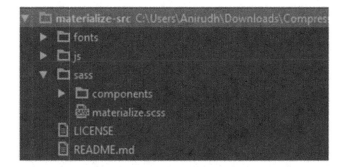

Figure 1-3. *Materialize SASS version content*

Sass is a pre-compiler language that cannot be directly used in a browser. In order to make it work in browser, you need to compile it and generate the CSS, which is browser friendly.

You will learn more about Sass in the later chapters where I will explain the process of including Sass in your Materialize projects.

Gallery

Figures 1-4 through 1-6 show the web sites of Gaggle Mail, Stamplay, and Jumpr, which were made using Materialize. You can see how material design principles when applied to these sites enhance the look and feel, thus providing appealing aesthetics and stunning design.

Figure 1-4. `https://gaggle.email/`

Figure 1-5. `https://stamplay.com/`

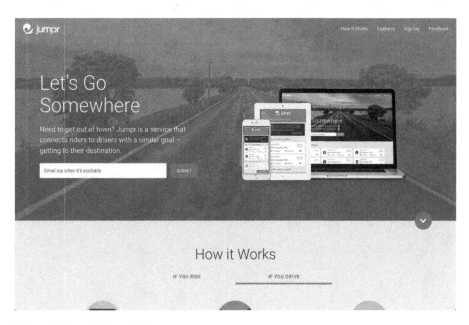

Figure 1-6. `www.jumpr.it/`

You can view many more of these web sites at `http://materializecss.com/showcase.html`.

Summary

In this chapter, you took a look at an overview of Material Design and the Materialize framework, which adheres to the Material Design concept. In the following chapters, you will learn more about the components, grid system, and various other aspects which help build faster, consistent, and attractive web sites. Meanwhile, apart from web sites, you can also use Materialize to build hybrid apps with a feel and look that will make them stand out from the crowd.

CHAPTER 2

■ ■ ■

Grid Fundamentals and Helper Classes

In the previous chapter, you took a look at the Material Design methodology and a basic overview of Materialize, a resourceful framework that adopts the Material Design concept. In this chapter, you will learn about the basic markup as well as the grid layout of the Materialize framework. Then you will learn about functions such as offsets, nesting of columns, and utility classes. You will also explore the responsiveness of the Materialize framework, which makes it a leading framework for web design and development.

Materialize Grid Explained

Responsiveness is vital, with almost all frameworks adhering to responsive web design concept. A responsive grid layout is imperative as it divides the screen in a multi-column structure. The positioning and deciding of the dimensions that a grid layout offers makes it an essential part of web design.

A grid layout helps achieve good readability, a high degree of flexibility, and page cohesiveness. Typically, a grid layout is composed of 12 columns that occupy the total screen width and scale depending on the size of the browser window. Materialize's 12-column grid helps create a powerful layout without the bulk or clutter associated with some of the heavy frameworks out there. It helps you lay out content in a highly organized manner.

With responsiveness baked in, you can use attributes such as nesting within columns, offsets, the push-and-pull pattern, and centering of grid columns to build interactive and aesthetically pleasing web sites.

Creating Responsive Layouts

Before proceeding with the grid layout, here are the terms used in creating responsive layouts with Materialize:

- **Row**: A horizontal container that spans the width of the web page (or the container width, if it is a nested row).

- **Column**: Vertical columns within a row; you can specify their width using classes.

© Anirudh Prabhu and Aravind Shenoy 2016
A. Prabhu and A. Shenoy, *Introducing Materialize*, DOI 10.1007/978-1-4842-2349-9_2

Materialize provides support for various screen sizes, similar to other frameworks like Bootstrap or foundation by means of class prefixes, which are as follows:

- **Small**: Classes meant for small screens (screens less than 600px in width). For example, if you assign a .s7 class to an element, that element will span across seven virtual columns on your mobile screen.

- **Medium**: Classes meant for medium-sized screens such as tablets (to be precise, for screens more than 600px and less than 992px in width). If you assign a .m7 class to an element, that element will span across seven columns on your tablet screen.

- **Large**: Classes meant for large screens such as desktops and laptops (to be precise, for screens more than 992px in width). If you assign a .l7 class to an element, that element will span across seven columns on your desktop or laptop screen.

	Small Devices <=600px	Medium-Sized Screen s<=992px	Large-Screen Devices >992px
Class Prefix	.s	.m	.l
Container	85%	85%	70%
Number of columns	12	12	12

.container Class

Materialize provides a *container* class that is not a part of the grid system but plays an important role for systematic layout of your web site. Think of it as a container in a real-world way wherein you can systematically store your elements, typically containing some child elements and enclosing the body content. It is a dummy div wrapper used for setting backgrounds and padding on another <div>.

The container class takes 70% of total window width and centers the page content, as depicted n Figure 2-1.

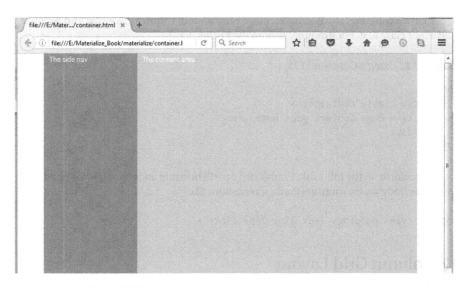

Figure 2-1. *The conatiner class*

Compare Figure 2-1 with Figure 2-2 to see the difference with and without the container class.

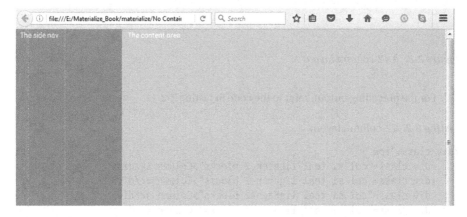

Figure 2-2. *Without the container class*

To use a container in Materialize, place your content within a <div> tag and assign a container class to it. For example, refer to the Listing 2-1.

Listing 2-1. Using a Container Class

```
<body>
      <div class="container">
        <!-- Page Content goes here -->
      </div>
</body>
```

Henceforth, in the following examples, you will be using an inline style for padding within the body tag for more aesthetic screenshots, like

```
<body  style="padding: 25px 25px 25px 25px;">
```

12-Column Grid Layout

Materialize's default grid has 12 columns of equal width, as depicted in Figure 2-3.

Figure 2-3. *A 12-column layout*

For the preceding output, refer to the code in Listing 2-2.

Listing 2-2. 12-column layout

```
<div class="row">
    <div class="col s1 teal lighten-2 blocks">Column 1</div>
    <div class="col s1 teal lighten-2 blocks">Column 2</div>
    <div class="col s1 teal lighten-2 blocks">Column 3</div>
    <div class="col s1 teal lighten-2 blocks">Column 4</div>
    <div class="col s1 teal lighten-2 blocks">Column 5</div>
    <div class="col s1 teal lighten-2 blocks">Column 6</div>
    <div class="col s1 teal lighten-2 blocks">Column 7</div>
    <div class="col s1 teal lighten-2 blocks">Column 8</div>
    <div class="col s1 teal lighten-2 blocks">Column 9</div>
    <div class="col s1 teal lighten-2 blocks">Column 10</div>
    <div class="col s1 teal lighten-2 blocks">Column 11</div>
    <div class="col s1 teal lighten-2 blocks">Column 12</div>
</div>
```

Columns Incorporated in Rows

You need to place all columns under a row class while building a layout. In Materialize, if there are more than 12 columns, the last element will be pushed to the next line.

Listing 2-3 shows the code that explains the concept better.

Listing 2-3. Columns Under a row Class

```
<div class="row">
        <div class="col s12 teal lighten-2 blocks">This div is 12-columns
        wide</div>
</div>
<div class="row">
        <div class="col s6 teal lighten-2 blocks">This div is 6-columns
        wide</div>
        <div class="col s6 teal lighten-2 blocks">This div is 6-columns
        wide</div>
</div>
```

In Listing 2-3, you assign the row class to the <div> element. Then you enclose a <div> and assign the col s12 class to it.

Remember that the Materialize framework is responsive and therefore col s12 stands for 12 columns on a small screen. Then you use the teal class in conjunction with the col s12 class. Since Material design is based on creating a real-world effect for web sites, you can lighten the teal color by using the lighten-2 class. In Materialize, you can darken or lighten the color; there are many immersive color palettes on the official documentation on their site.

Moving forward, you create another <div> and assign the row class to it. You then use two <div>s, each of six columns, each using the col s6 class. Then you assign a teal color with a lightened shade similar to the <div> you created for the first part of the Listing. Close the <div> for the second row class.

The output will be as shown in Figure 2-4. It shows an example of dividing 12 columns into two sets, each containing 6 columns in a row.

Figure 2-4. *12 columns into two sets*

Offsets

Sometimes, you may need a space between elements which may be equal to certain number of columns. Materialize provides the ability to offset some elements, eliminating the need to do so manually. You can move columns to the right, meaning pushing them for more spacing.

Let's understand this means by of an example; see Listing 2-4.

Listing 2-4. Offsets

```
<div class="row">
      <div class="col s12 teal lighten-2 blocks">This div is 12-columns
      wide on all screen sizes</div>
</div>
<div class="row">
      <div class="col s6 offset-s6 teal lighten-2 blocks">6-columns
      (offset-by-6) </div>
</div>
```

In Listing 2-4, you create a 12-column layout in a row and use the light teal color for the columns. Next, you create another row of 6 columns and assign the same light teal color to it. However, you use an offset-s6 class along with the col s6 class.

Offsets in Materialize are added using the offset-sn class wherein s is used for small screen followed by n, which is the number of columns to be offset. In Listing 2-4, you use offset-s6, which will offset the element by six columns to the right.

The output of the code is shown in Figure 2-5.

Figure 2-5. *Offsets on screen*

Push and Pull

Push and Pull can be used to change the order of the columns. Materialize uses the push-sn class and pull-sn class for pushing and pulling the order of columns. The push-sn class pushes the element by n columns whereas the pull-sn class pulls the column by n columns, where s stands for small screens and n is the number of columns the element will be pushed or pulled depending on the requirement. Refer to Listing 2-5 for an example.

Listing 2-5. Push and Pull

```
<div class="">
    <div class="row">
        <div class="col s9 push-s3 teal lighten-2 blocks"> PUSH: to the
        Right </div>
        <div class="col s3 pull-s9 teal lighten-2 blocks"> PULL: to the Left
        </div>
    </div>
</div>
```

In Listing 2-5, you push the columns to the right using the push-s3 class and you pull the columns to the left using the pull-s9 class. The push and pull classes are used in conjunction with the col class.

The output of the code can be seen in Figure 2-6.

Figure 2-6. *Push and pull on screen*

Adding Responsiveness

In previous examples, you saw the use of col sn (such as col s5, col s6, etc.) wherein s stands for small screen size. This means that it is a fixed layout wherein the rules will be propagated upwards. By specifying sn, you define that the columns will occupy n columns on all screen sizes (small, medium, and large screen sizes). For example, col s6 will result in six columns on a small screen or any size larger than the small screen. However, you can explicitly set the responsiveness based on the screen sizes.

Let's understand this by looking at Listing 2-6.

Listing 2-6. Adding Responsiveness

```
<div class="row">
        <div class="grid-example col s12 teal lighten-2 blocks">I am full-
        width on all screens(col s12)</div>
    </div>
    <div class="row">
        <div class="grid-example col s12 m6 teal lighten-2 blocks">I am
        full-width on small screens (col s12 m6)</div>
    </div>
```

In Listing 2-6, you create two rows. In the first row, you assign the col s12 class, which means that it will span across 12 columns on small, medium, and large screen sizes.

However, in the second row, you use the col s12 m6 class, which means that the content will span across 12 columns on small-sized screen and only 6 columns on medium-sized screens.

Refer to Figure 2-7 to see the output on a medium-sized screen.

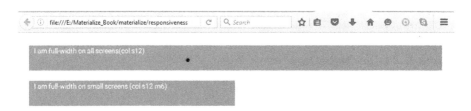

Figure 2-7. *Responsive design*

If you decrease the browser screen size to simulate a small screen or view the web page on a small screen, the second block, which spanned across 6 columns on a medium-sized screen, will span across all 12 columns for the small screen, as depicted in Figure 2-8.

Figure 2-8. *Resizing for a smaller screen*

Responsive Side Navigation Layout

You can also build immersive layouts that will resize and rearrange the content. In this section, you will build a responsive side navigation layout, which resizes and rearranges the content depending on the screen size. See Listing 2-7.

Listing 2-7. Responsive Side Navigation Layout

```
<!DOCTYPE html>
<html>
<head>
    <!--Import Google Icon Font-->
    <link href="http://fonts.googleapis.com/icon?family=Material+Icons"
    rel="stylesheet">
    <!--Import materialize.css-->
    <link type="text/css" rel="stylesheet" href="css/materialize.min.
    css"  media="screen,projection"/>
    <!--Let browser know website is optimized for mobile-->
```

```html
    <meta name="viewport" content="width=device-width, initial-scale=1.0"/>
    <style>
        .blocks{
            height:50px;
            outline: 1px solid #fff;
            color:#fff;
        }
        .fullLength{
            height: 100vh;
        }
        @media screen and (max-width: 600px){
            .fullLength{
                height: auto;
            }
        }
    </style>
</head>
<body  style="padding: 25px 25px 25px 25px;">
<!--Import jQuery before materialize.js-->
<script type="text/javascript" src="https://code.jquery.com/jquery-
2.1.1.min.js"></script>
<script type="text/javascript" src="js/materialize.min.js"></script>

    <div class="row">

        <div class="col s12 m2 lime accent-4 fullLength" style="color:
        #ffff">
            <a href="#" style="color: #000;display:block;font-size:
            18px;">Link 1</a>
            <a href="#" style="color: #000;display:block;font-size:
            18px;">Link 2</a>
            <a href="#" style="color: #000;display:block;font-size:
            18px;">Link 3</a>
        </div>

        <div class="col s12 m10 teal lighten-10 fullLength" style="color:
        #fff">
            <p>Far far away, behind the word mountains, far from the
            countries Vokalia and Consonantia, there live the blind texts.
            Separated they live in Bookmarksgrove right at the coast of
            the Semantics, a large language ocean. A small river named
            Duden flows by their place and supplies it with the necessary
            regelialia. It is a paradisematic country, in which roasted
            parts of sentences fly into your mouth. Even the all-powerful
            Pointing has no control about the blind texts it is an almost
            unorthographic life One day however a small line of blind text
            by the name of Lorem Ipsum decided to leave for the far World of
            Grammar.s</p>
```

```
        </div>
    </div>
</body>
</html>
```

In Listing 2-7, initially you create a <div> element containing three links. The <div> element spans across 12 columns on the small screen and 2 columns on medium and large screens. You assign the color lime for this <div> and assign the .fullLength class to the <div>.

Similarly, you create another <div> that spans across 12 columns on the small screen and 10 columns on a medium-sized screen. You add content within the second <div>. You assign the color teal for this <div>. Similar to the first example, you assign the fullLength class to this <div>.

Both the <div>s are enclosed in a row.

In the <head> section of the preceding code, you assign the height for the .fullLength class. You define a media query, too.

Upon executing the code, you will see the output shown in Figure 2-9.

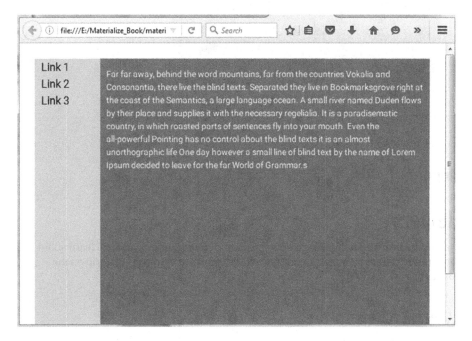

Figure 2-9. *Output*

As you can see from Figure 2-9, there is a side navigation panel wherein you can see Link 1, Link 2, and Link 3 hyperlinks. You can also see the content in teal to the right of the side navigation.

21

On a small screen, the links are stacked above the content, as displayed in Figure 2-10.

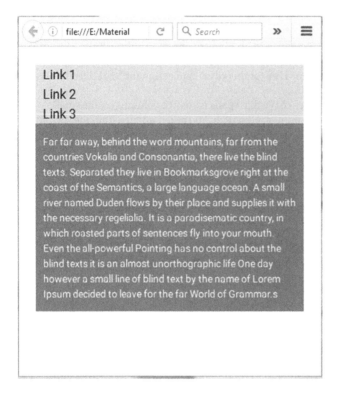

Figure 2-10. *Links on top*

Helpers

Materialize provides helper classes for common UI requirements. You will learn about these utility classes by means of several code examples to help you get a grip on the concepts.

Vertical Align

The vertical align function involves centering the elements within a container. You use the valign-wrapper class for aligning the content vertically. Let's understand this by means of an example. See Listing 2-8.

Listing 2-8. Vertical Align

```
<div class="row">
    <div class="valign-wrapper grey darken-2 col m6" style="height: 300px;">
        <p class="valign teal lighten-2" style="color: #FFF;">Far far away,
        behind the word mountains, far from the countries Vokalia and
        Consonantia, there live the blind texts. Separated they live in
        Bookmarksgrove right at the coast of the Semantics, a large language
        ocean. A small river named Duden flows by their place and supplies
        it with the necessary regelialia.</p>
    </div>
</div>
```

In Listing 2-8, you create a container using the valign-wrapper property spanning across six columns on a medium-size screen. You also assign the height of 300 pixels to it and use the dark grey color. You assign the valign property to the content within the paragraph <p> tags. You also assign the teal color to the content inside the same <p> tags.

The output of the content is depicted in Figure 2-11.

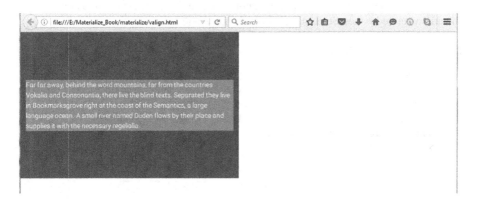

Figure 2-11. *Verical alignment on screen*

Text Alignment

Text alignment is a common requirement to position text content on the layout. In Materialize, you use the left-align, right-align, and center-align classes to align the content on the left, right, and center of the screen respectively. For an example, see Listing 2-9.

Listing 2-9. Text Alignment

```
<div class="row">
    <p class="left-align">Left Aligned: To the left</p>
    <p class="right-align">Right Aligned: Always Right</p>
    <p class="center-align"> In the Center </p>
</div>
```

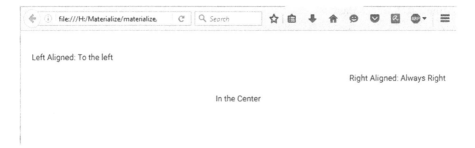

Figure 2-12. *Text alignment on screen*

Quick Floats

Floating an element is one of the most common operations. Float classes help you define the float behavior. Instead of writing floats in CSS for every required element, you can use the classes provided by Materialize to do so.

A point to keep in mind here is that Materialize uses !important to avoid any specificity related issues. See Listing 2-10 and Figure 2-13.

Listing 2-10. Floating Text

```
<div class="row">
    <div class="left grey darken-2" style="color: #FFF;padding: 10px;">Float
to the left</div>
    <div class="right teal darken-2" style="color: #fff;padding:
    10px;">Float to the right</div>
</div>
```

Figure 2-13. *Floating text on screen*

Hiding Content

Materialize provides an easy way to hide elements on all screens or on specific screen sizes by providing helper classes for the same. See Table 2-1 for the classes.

Table 2-1. *Hiding Content*

	Screen Range
.hide	Hidden for all Devices
.hide-on-small-only	Hidden for Mobile Only
.hide-on-med-only	Hidden for Tablet Only
.hide-on-med-and-down	Hidden for Tablet and Below
.hide-on-med-and-up	Hidden for Tablet and Above
.hide-on-large-only	Hidden for Desktop Only

The .hide-on-small-only class is used when the content needs to be hidden only on the small screen, meaning you will be able to see the content on medium or large screens. The .hide-on-med-only class is used when the content needs to be hidden on medium screens only. Similarly, in Listing 2-11, you use the .hide-on-large-only class, which means the content will be hidden on large and extra-large screens.

Listing 2-11. Hiding Content

```
<div class="row">
    <p class="hide-on-med-and-down" style="font-size: 20px;">Web Design</p>
    <p class="hide-on-large-only" style="font-size: 20px;">Big Data</p>
</div>
```

In Listing 2-11, the content Web Design is assigned the hide-on-med-and-down class, meaning it will be visible on only large screens but will not be visible on the small and medium screens.

Similarly, the content Big Data is assigned the hide-on-large-only class, meaning it will be visible on small and medium screens and not on the large screens.

On executing the code, the output shown in Figure 2-14 is generated on medium and large-sized screens.

Web Design

Figure 2-14. *Output on medium and large screens*

As defined in the code, Figure 2-14 displays the content "Web Design" on a large screen. However, when you see the output on a small screen, "Web Design" cannot be seen. Instead, you can see the content "Big Data" as defined in the code. See Figure 2-15.

Figure 2-15. *Output on a small screen*

Truncation

Materialize provides helpers to handle text truncation. For truncating lengthy text with an ellipsis, just add the class truncate to the required element. This is demonstrated Listing 2-12 and Figure 2-16.

Listing 2-12. Truncating

```
<div class="row">
    <div class="valign-wrapper grey darken-2 col m6" style="height: 300px;">
        <h5 class="valign lime accent-4 truncate" style="padding: 10px">
Far far away, behind the word mountains, far from the countries Vokalia
and Consonantia, there live the blind texts. Separated they live in
Bookmarksgrove right at the coast of the Semantics, a large language ocean.
A small river named Duden flows by their place and supplies it with the
necessary regelialia.
```

```
</h5>
    </div>
</div>
```

In Listing 2-12, you create a row and then you use the `valign-wrapper` class for the `<div>` element inside that row for vertical alignment. You define `<h5>` tags within that `<div>` and place the content within the `<h5>` tags. You then use the `valign` class to vertically align the content, followed by assigning the `truncate` class to the same `<h5>` tag in addition to defining the lime color.

Upon executing the code, the output displays the truncated text instead of the entire paragraph, as depicted in Figure 2-16.

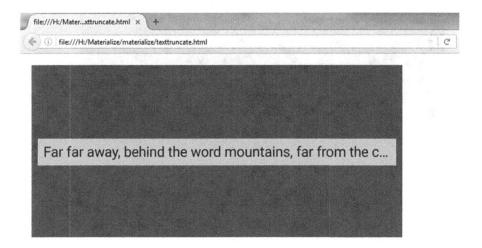

Figure 2-16. *Truncated text on screen*

Hoverable

The Hoverable feature provided by Materialize adds an animation for displaying the box shadows. This is achieved by simple addition of the `hoverable` class to the desired element. This is demonstrated with Listing 2-13 and Figure 2-17. In Listing 2-13, you use the code from previous example and insert the `hoverable` class into it.

Figure 2-17. *Hoverable on screen*

Listing 2-13. Hoverable Code

```
<div class="valign-wrapper grey lighten-3 hoverable" style="padding:
10px;display: inline-block">
        <img src="images/sample.jpg" class="valign"/>
    </div>
```

Summary

In this chapter, you took a look at the grid layout and other grid attributes. You also reviewed the concepts of visibility and utility classes. You then took a look at positioning of columns by offsets, push and pull, and so on.

In the next chapter, you will look at some more building blocks of this framework like color palettes, making images and videos responsive, adding depth to an element, styling tables, and typography.

CHAPTER 3

■ ■ ■

Beyond Fundamentals

In the previous chapter, you took a look at the Materialize grid system for responsive design and development. You also looked at the helper classes provided by Materialize for regular UI requirements such as floating elements, vertically aligning the elements, and toggling the visibility of the elements.

In this chapter, you will look at the various CSS utilities such as

- Color Palette
- Responsive Images and Videos
- Shadows
- Tables
- Typography

Color Palette

Materialize provides a material design based color palette as part of the package. Each color in the palette comes in dual variations, light or dark, to create an immersive experience. These variations can be applied by using the `lighten-x` or `darken-x` classes (where x stands for the intensity of the color variation). These palettes are shown in Figure 3-1.

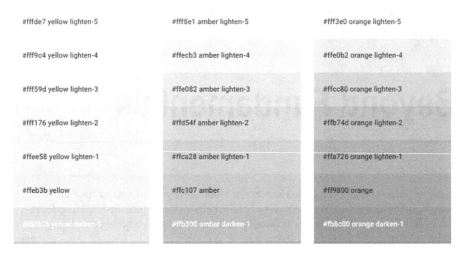

Figure 3-1. Palettes

To apply a color as the background, use the class for the specific color, for example amber, in conjunction with the light or dark classes, along with the intensity, for example lighten-2. Listing 3-1 shows the code snippet for the same.

Listing 3-1. Applying a Color to the Background

```
<div class="card-panel amber lighten-2">This is an element with an amber
background and additional lighten-2 class</div>
```

In Listing 3-1, you use a card-panel class within a <div> element followed by the amber color for the card-panel and the lighten-2 class to add the texture and intensity, respectively.

The output of the code on execution is shown in Figure 3-2.

Figure 3-2. A colored background

In order to apply color to only the text in the content, append -text to the color class, such as amber-text. Further on you will use the lighten-2 class on the text to adjust the lightness and intensity.

Listing 3-2 shows the code for creating a heading 5, <h5>, class and adding content to it. You use the amber-text class along with the lighten-2 class.

Listing 3-2. Adding Content

```
<h5 class="amber-text lighten-2">This is an element with an amber background
and additional lighten-2 class</h5>
```

The output of the code on execution will color the text only, as depicted in Figure 3-3.

Figure 3-3. Adding content

Responsive Images

Responsive images are an important component of responsive web design (RWD). In the early days of web design, designers used to develop separate web sites for various devices. However, with mobiles and tablets of various makes and sizes flooding the market, building different web sites for different devices has become quite difficult. Responsive web design adopts a one-site-fits-all approach and is device agnostic. The approach for responsiveness in images in Materialize is quite simple: just deliver the pixels that the device can actually use. In Materialize, you need to add the responsive-img class to the image tag. Adding this class will result in changes to the CSS attributes with the image's max-width set to 100% and height to auto. See Listing 3-3 for an example.

Listing 3-3. Responsive Images

```
<img class="responsive-img" src="images/abstract-mosaic-background.png">
```

As you can see, you add the responsive-img class to the <img> tag. The output of the code on execution can be seen in the following two images where Figure 3-4 depicts the output in a normal web browser window and Figure 3-5 on a resized small screen.

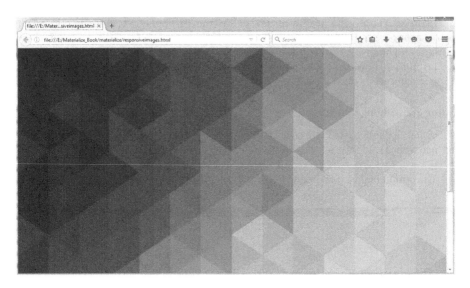

Figure 3-4. *Normal web browser window*

Figure 3-5. *Smaller window*

Rounded Images

With the introduction of border-radius, the Web has gotten a lot less square. To create a rounded border in Materialize, you apply the circle class to an element.

In Listing 3-4, you create a <div> and enclose an image inside it using the <img> tag. You use a picture of Miami and add the circle class to it. For the example, use the image in Figure 3-6, which you name as Miami.

Figure 3-6. Miami

Listing 3-4. Rounding the Edges

```
<div class="row" style="margin-top: 10px;margin-left: 10px">
   <p><img src="images/miami.png" class="circle"></p>
</div>
```

On executing the code, the borders of the image are rounded. Figure 3-7 depicts the resulting image.

Figure 3-7. Rounded edges

Responsive Embeds

There are a few HTML elements that do not go hand-in-hand with responsive layouts. An example of this is the good old IFrame, which is an important aspect, considering that you can embed content from external sources such as YouTube.

Services such as YouTube and Vimeo provide code that you can copy and paste into your own web site to embed content. It's recommended that you host video with YouTube because it will save server space and it will display the video appropriately, irrespective of the user's browser or device.

When you embed content from an external source, the code will include an IFrame. This IFrame enables external content to be displayed on your web site because it includes a URL that points to the source of the streamed content.

In Materialize, you can add responsiveness to embedded videos by wrapping them in a <div> with the video-container class. Using this class results in setting the width of the media to embed 100% and height to auto.

In Listing 3-5, you add the video-container class to the <div> in conjunction with the row class. You define an IFrame and allocate a width of 560 and height of 315. You also assign the allowfullscreen attribute to the same <iframe> tag.

Listing 3-5. Embedding a Video

```
<div class="row video-container" style="margin-top: 10px;margin-left: 10px">
    <iframe width="560" height="315" src="https://www.youtube.com/embed/
    u7v5vzHPi8I" frameborder="0" allowfullscreen></iframe>
</div>
```

The output of the code on a normal desktop screen and small screen can be seen in Figures 3-8 and Figure 3-9. This defines the responsiveness for embedded videos in Materialize.

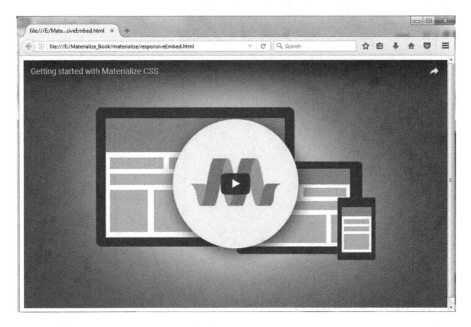

Figure 3-8. *Responsive embed on a desktop screen*

Figure 3-9. *Responsive embed on a small screen*

Responsive Videos

Video content is crucial in today's era wherein the video medium is the most sought by users worldwide. But it is a challenge to add responsiveness to video content given the advent of responsive and fluid layouts. Videos can be hosted on your site; alternatively, you can use HTML5's `<video>` tag. In Materialize, all you need to do is add a `video-container` class to the parent `<div>`. Then you add the `responsive-video` class to the `<video>` tag to make your videos responsive. Listing 3-6 shows the way to make videos responsive.

Listing 3-6. Responsive Video

```
<div class="row video-container" style="margin-top: 10px;margin-left: 10px">
    <video class="responsive-video" controls>
        <source src="movie.mp4" type="video/mp4">
    </video>
</div>
```

You use a parent `<div>` and assign the `video-container` class to the `<div>` element. Then you use the `<video>` tag and assign the `responsive-video` class to it. You include the location and file format of the `<video>` in the `<source>` tag. See Figure 3-10.

Figure 3-10. *A screenshot of repsonsive video*

Shadows

To create an immersive experience, certain things must be displayed as they would look in real life. To create shadows for an image or content, you use the `z-depth` class to determine how raised or close the element is on the page.

Listing 3-7 contains the code snippet to demonstrate the shadow effect.

Listing 3-7. The Shadow Effect

```
<div class="row">
    <p class="z-depth-1 amber accent-3 col m2" style="height: 100px">z-
    depth-1</p>
    <p class="z-depth-2 amber accent-3 col m2" style="height: 100px">z-
    depth-2</p>
    <p class="z-depth-3 amber accent-3 col m2" style="height: 100px">z-
    depth-3</p>
    <p class="z-depth-4 amber accent-3 col m2" style="height: 100px">z-
    depth-4</p>
    <p class="z-depth-5 amber accent-3 col m2" style="height: 100px">z-
    depth-5</p>
</div>
```

In Listing 3-7, you use a parent <div> element and enclose content in five <p> tags. Each <p> element spans across two columns on a medium-size screen and you add the z-depth class to each one. However, you append a number that determines the intensity of the shadow to each z-depth class. For example, you used the z-depth-1 class for the first <p> element, followed by the z-depth-2 class for the second <p> tag, and so on. You assign the same amber color for each <p> element. See the results in Figure 3-11.

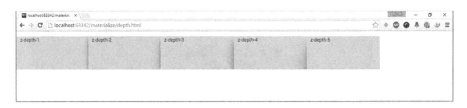

Figure 3-11. *Shadows*

Tables

A table is an optimal way to organize a huge amount of related data. Materialize provides a few utility classes that help streamline the appearance of your tables. An important aspect is the automatic centering of the tables on small screens.

You create a table the same way you use in normal HTML. Listing 3-8 contains the snippet for the table using HTML tags. Tables in Materialize are borderless by default.

Listing 3-8. A Table

```
<h1>Catalog</h1>
    <table>
        <thead>
        <tr>
            <th data-field="product">Product</th>
            <th data-field="availableQuantity">Quantity</th>
            <th data-field="price">Price for an unit</th>
```

```
    </tr>
    </thead>
    <tbody>
    <tr>
        <td>Apples</td>
        <td>10</td>
        <td>$0.87</td>
    </tr>
    <tr>
        <td>Mango</td>
        <td>5</td>
        <td>$3.76</td>
    </tr>
    <tr>
        <td>Oranges</td>
        <td>3</td>
        <td>$7.00</td>
    </tr>
    </tbody>
</table>
```

On executing the code, the output will be displayed as depicted in Figure 3-12.

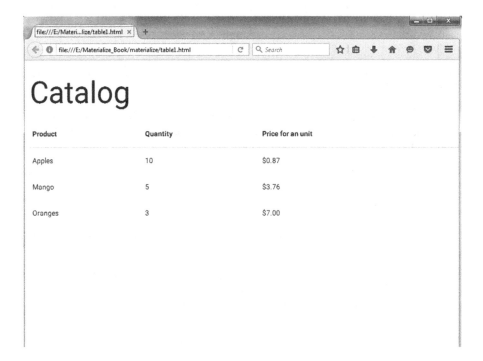

Figure 3-12. A table

As you can see, you have built a simple catalog table. Since tables are borderless in Materialize, you need to add the `bordered` class to the `table` tag to create a bordered table. The output of the code after adding the `bordered` class is shown in Figure 3-13.

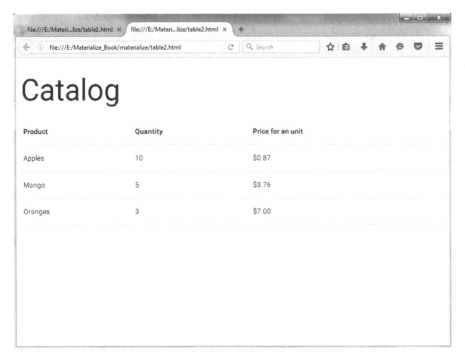

Figure 3-13. *A bordered table*

Adding the `bordered` class to the table gives a border below every row. However, if you replace the `bordered` class with the `striped` class, you get a striped table; see Figure 3-14.

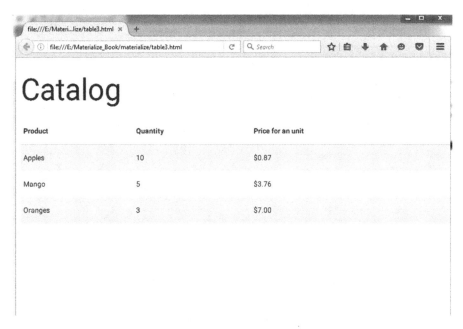

Figure 3-14. *A striped table*

Highlighting of rows on hover can be established by adding the highlight class to the table. Let's replace the striped class with highlight. You will see a borderless table as per the norm. However, when you hover over any row, that row darkens, akin to getting highlighted. Figure 3-15 depicts the output when you hover on the first row.

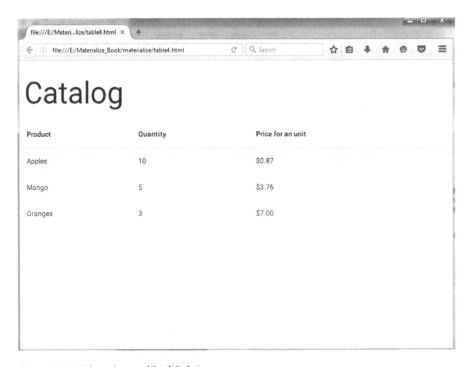

Figure 3-15. *Hovering and highlighting*

If you add only the centered class to the table, the content would adjust in the middle of the page, as depicted in Figure 3-16.

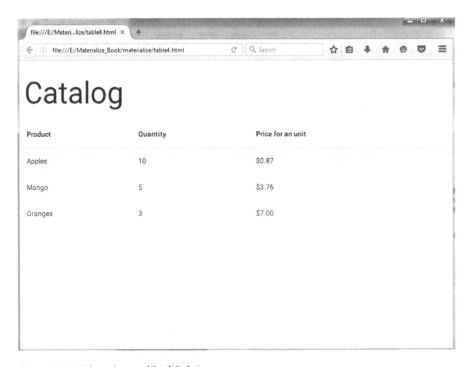

Figure 3-16. *Centered content*

Another aspect is the responsiveness of the table. If you add a `responsive-table` class to the `<table>` tag, it will result in a responsive table when the browser is resized. Let's see the output on a normal screen, as depicted in Figure 3-17. The output on a smaller screen is shown in Figure 3-18.

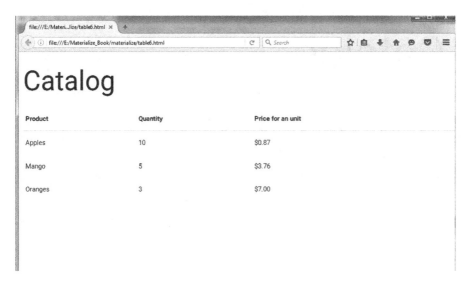

Figure 3-17. *Output on a desktop screen*

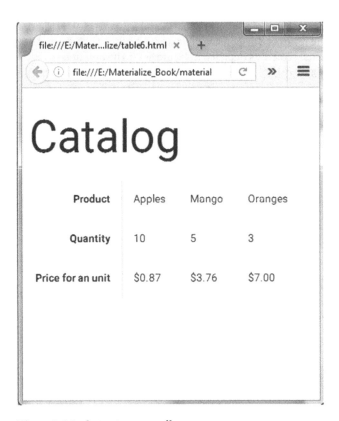

Figure 3-18. *Output on a smaller screen*

As you can see from Figures 3-17 and 3-18, the table resizes based on the size of the browser. There is even a difference in the position of the rows and columns.

Typography

Materialize's typography delivers pleasing web design and clean coding with minimalist site structures designed for easy readability. Materalize uses the Roboto font as the default font. It supports the latest version of the Roboto font with five different variations and font weights, namely 200, 300, 400, 500, and 600.

You can get a preview of the Roboto font at https://fonts.google.com/specimen/Roboto and in Figure 3-19.

Roboto font Preview
Roboto font Preview
Roboto font Preview
Roboto font Preview
Roboto font Preview
Roboto font Preview
Roboto font Preview
Roboto font Preview
Roboto font Preview
Roboto font Preview
Roboto font Preview
Roboto font Preview

Figure 3-19. *The Roboto font*

You can override the default Roboto font for your web page by changing the font stack in your CSS stylesheet. The following is an example of overriding those fonts:

```
html {
    font-family: Gill Sans, Calibri, Trebuchet, sans-serif;
  }
```

You can replace the font family as per the requirement by entering the relevant font family in the preceding code.

Blockquotes

Blockquotes are used to emphasize, isolate, or highlight portions of text on a web site. Listing 3-9 shows an example of a blockquote.

Listing 3-9. A blockquote

```
<div class="row">
<blockquote>
Lorem ipsum dolor sit amet, consectetur adipiscing elit. Nam de summo mox,
ut dixi, videbimus et ad id explicandum disputationem omnem conferemus.
At, si voluptas esset bonum, desideraret. Quippe: habes enim a rhetoribus;
Maximus dolor, inquit, brevis est. Istam voluptatem perpetuam quis potest
praestare sapienti? Itaque ad tempus ad Pisonem omnes. Expectoque quid ad
id, quod quaerebam, respondeas. Duo Reges: constructio interrete.
</blockquote>
</div>
```

Upon executing the code in Listing 3-9, the output will be as displayed in Figure 3-20.

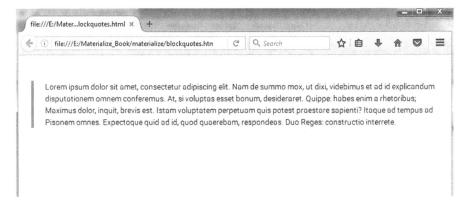

Figure 3-20. A blockquote

Materialize's `batteries-included` attributes are not limited to responsive grid layout but also enhance the feel by changing the font size and line spacing of the content, resulting in an awesome user experience.

Listing 3-10 shows an example of the flow-text feature. All you need to do is add the `flow-text` class to the content, and the font size and line spacing will adjust themselves based on the viewport.

Listing 3-10. The flow-text Class

```
<div class="row">
    <p class="flow-text">Lorem ipsum dolor sit amet, consectetur
    adipiscing elit. Nam de summo mox, ut dixi, videbimus et ad id
    explicandum disputationem omnem conferemus. At, si voluptas esset
    bonum, desideraret. Quippe: habes enim a rhetoribus; Maximus dolor,
    inquit, brevis est. Istam voluptatem perpetuam quis potest praestare
    sapienti? Itaque ad tempus ad Pisonem omnes. Expectoque quid ad id, quod
    quaerebam, respondeas. Duo Reges: constructio interrete. </p>
</div>
```

In Listing 3-10, you use the `flow-text` class for the `<p>` tag containing some generic content. Figure 3-21 shows the result.

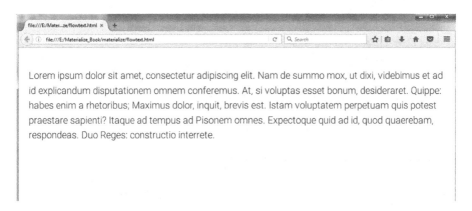

Figure 3-21. *The flow-text class in action*

If you reduce the size of the browser window to simulate the content on a small screen, you will see that the font size and spacing reduces proportionally yet is clear, thereby resulting in an effective user experience. See Figure 3-22.

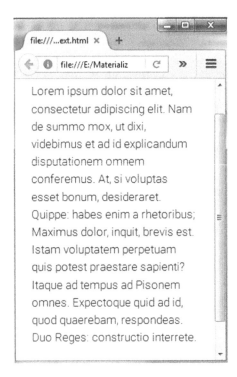

Figure 3-22. *The flow-text class on a smaller screen*

Summary

In this chapter, you looked at additional basic components of this framework, like the color palette, and how to use them. You also looked into how you can add videos and images using classes provided by Materialize. You also explored the responsive typography provided by Materialize.

In the next chapter, you will be looking at some JavaScript-based aspects of this framework.

CHAPTER 4

■ ■ ■

Materialize JavaScript

In the previous chapters, you explored some important building blocks and CSS-based components in Materialize. In this chapter, you will take a look at JavaScript-powered components in Materialize and their implementation in a hands-on manner.

You will look at the following topics in this chapter:

- Collapsible
- Toasts and Tooltips
- Dropdowns
- Modal
- ScrollFire and ScrollSpy
- SideNav
- Tabs
- Waves
- Transitions
- Carousel

Collapsible

Accordion helps you encapsulate a large amount of content in a compact area. Accordions are styled like a stack of collapsible panels and act like a multi-level menu. Accordion menus are an important solution when you are pressed for space on your web site. Collapsibles are accordion elements that expand when they are clicked.

Listing 4-1 shows an example of a Collapsible.

Listing 4-1. Creating a Simple Collapsible Structure

```
<!DOCTYPE html>
<html>
<head>
    <!--Import Google Icon Font-->
    <link href="http://fonts.googleapis.com/icon?family=Material+Icons"
    rel="stylesheet">
```

```
    <!--Import materialize.css-->
    <link type="text/css" rel="stylesheet" href="https://cdnjs.
    cloudflare.com/ajax/libs/materialize/0.97.7/css/materialize.min.
    css"  media="screen,projection"/>

    <!--Let browser know website is optimized for mobile-->
    <meta name="viewport" content="width=device-width, initial-scale=1.0"/>
    <style>

    </style>
</head>

<body style="padding:25px">
<!--Import jQuery before materialize.js-->
<script type="text/javascript" src="https://code.jquery.com/jquery-
2.1.1.min.js"></script>
<script type="text/javascript" src="https://cdnjs.cloudflare.com/ajax/libs/
materialize/0.97.7/js/materialize.min.js"></script>
<div class="row">
    <h1 class=" deep-orange-text darken-3">Materialize Training Session</h1>
    <h3>17/09/2016</h3>
    <ul class="collapsible" data-collapsible="accordion">
        <li>
            <div class="collapsible-header">Event Details</div>
            <div class="collapsible-body"><p>Lorem ipsum dolor sit amet,
            consectetuer adipiscing elit. Aenean commodo ligula eget
            dolor. Aenean massa. Cum sociis natoque penatibus et magnis
            dis parturient montes, nascetur ridiculus mus. Donec quam
            felis, ultricies nec, pellentesque eu, pretium quis, sem. Nulla
            consequat massa quis enim. Donec pede justo, fringilla vel,
            aliquet nec, vulputate eget, arcu. In enim justo, rhoncus ut,
            imperdiet a, venenatis vitae, justo. Nullam dictum felis eu pede
            mollis pretium. Integer tincidunt.</p></div>
        </li>
        <li>
            <div class="collapsible-header">Speakers</div>
            <div class="collapsible-body">
                <ul>
                <li><i class="material-icons">speaker_notes</i> Anirudh
Prabhu.</li>
                <li><i class="material-icons">speaker_notes</i> Aravind
Shenoy.</li>
                </ul>
            </div>
        </li>
    </ul>

</div>
</body>
</html>
```

Upon executing the code, you will see two menus, Event Details and Speakers. When you click any of the menus, in this case, Event Details, you will reveal the content in that accordion (see Figure 4-1).

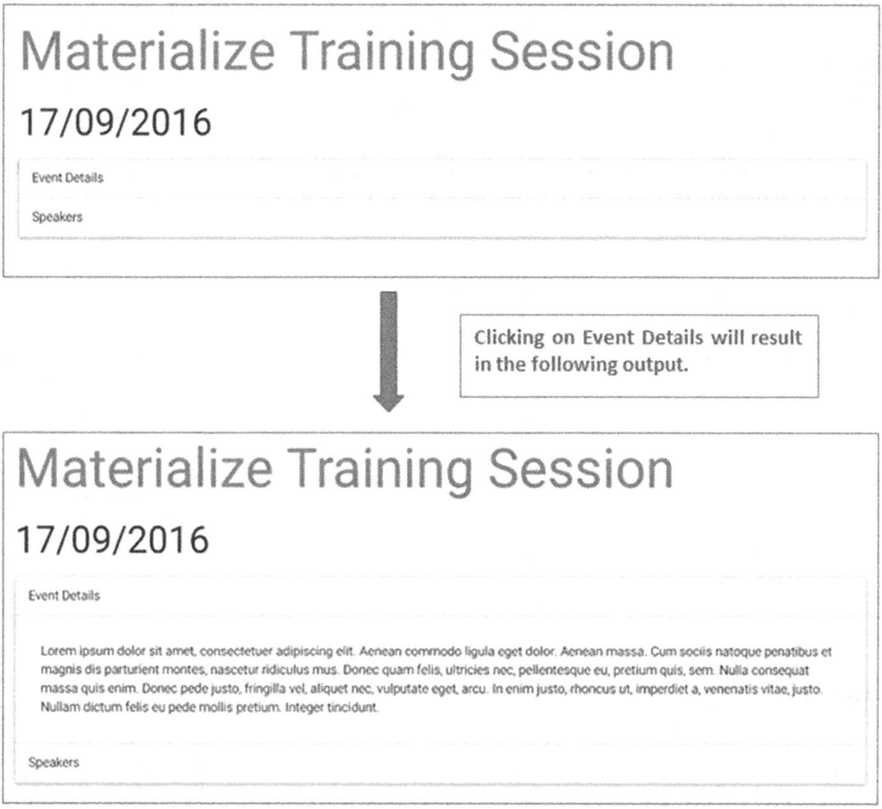

Figure 4-1. *Creating simple collapsible structure*

Let's understand how the output is generated by creating an example page for the Materialize training event.

In the above example, you first create a header using the <h1> tags for the Materialize Training event. Then, you use the <h3> tag to define the date for the Materialize Training event.

Next, you create the collapsible content using the list tags (<ul> and <li>). In the first list item, you assign the collapsible class and added the data-collapsible attribute to which you assigned the accordion value. Then the title for the collapsible is defined using the collapsible-header class. The header content acts like a button which, upon clicking, will unveil the content. Then you define the hidden content using the collapsible-body class.

Beyond this standard accordion, which simply collapses and expands, Materialize also provides different variations such as popout class, which will essentially display the element slightly larger and lifted, giving it a feel as if it is popping out of the flow.

To use the popout effect in your collapsible, add the popout class to the <ul> tag in conjunction with the collapsible class assigned to it, as shown in Listing 4-2.

Listing 4-2. Implementing the Popout Collapsible

```
<ul class="collapsible popout" data-collapsible="accordion">
```

When you click on Event Details, you will see the popup effect wherein it seems a bit lifted and pronounced compared to the normal result; see Figure 4-2.

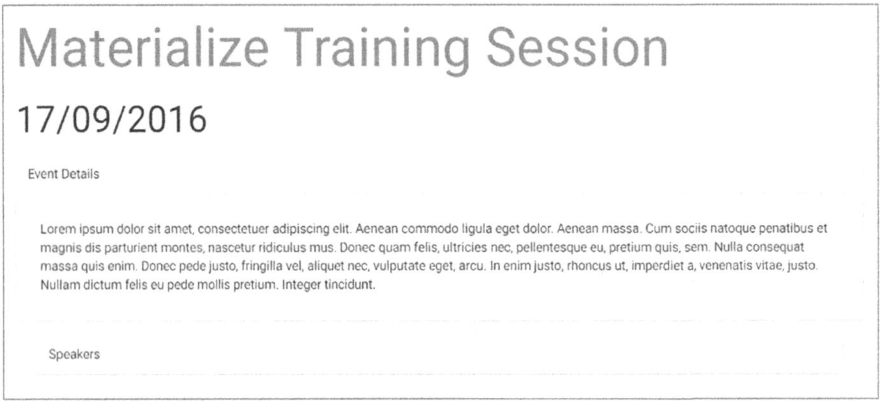

Materialize Training Session
17/09/2016

Event Details

Lorem ipsum dolor sit amet, consectetuer adipiscing elit. Aenean commodo ligula eget dolor. Aenean massa. Cum sociis natoque penatibus et magnis dis parturient montes, nascetur ridiculus mus. Donec quam felis, ultricies nec, pellentesque eu, pretium quis, sem. Nulla consequat massa quis enim. Donec pede justo, fringilla vel, aliquet nec, vulputate eget, arcu. In enim justo, rhoncus ut, imperdiet a, venenatis vitae, justo. Nullam dictum felis eu pede mollis pretium. Integer tincidunt.

Speakers

Figure 4-2. *Implementing a popout collapsible*

It is possible to keep one of the accordions open by using the active class in conjunction with the collapsible-header class. This will result in the specific accordion opening when you execute the code. Listing 4-3 contains the line of code where you need to include the active class. See Figure 4-3 for the results.

Listing 4-3. Active Accordion

```
<div class="collapsible-header active"> Event Details</div>
```

Materialize Training Session
17/09/2016

Event Details

Lorem ipsum dolor sit amet, consectetuer adipiscing elit. Aenean commodo ligula eget dolor. Aenean massa. Cum sociis natoque penatibus et magnis dis parturient montes, nascetur ridiculus mus. Donec quam felis, ultricies nec, pellentesque eu, pretium quis, sem. Nulla consequat massa quis enim. Donec pede justo, fringilla vel, aliquet nec, vulputate eget, arcu. In enim justo, rhoncus ut, imperdiet a, venenatis vitae, justo. Nullam dictum felis eu pede mollis pretium. Integer tincidunt.

Speakers

Figure 4-3. *Active accordion*

By default, only one panel of collapsible content will be visible at a given point of time. However, to keep multiple panels open, you can use the expandable value to the data-collapsible attribute.

Listing 4-4 shows the line of code that contains the expandable value for the data-collapsible attribute in conjunction with the collapsible class.

Listing 4-4. The expandable Value

```
<ul class="collapsible" data-collapsible="expandable">
```

Initially, you get an output that will have the first collapsible content (i.e. Event Details) open. If you click Speakers, it will show the content, but in this case the accordion content for both menus will be open, opposed to the default option where expanding one will result in the closing of the other. See Figure 4-4.

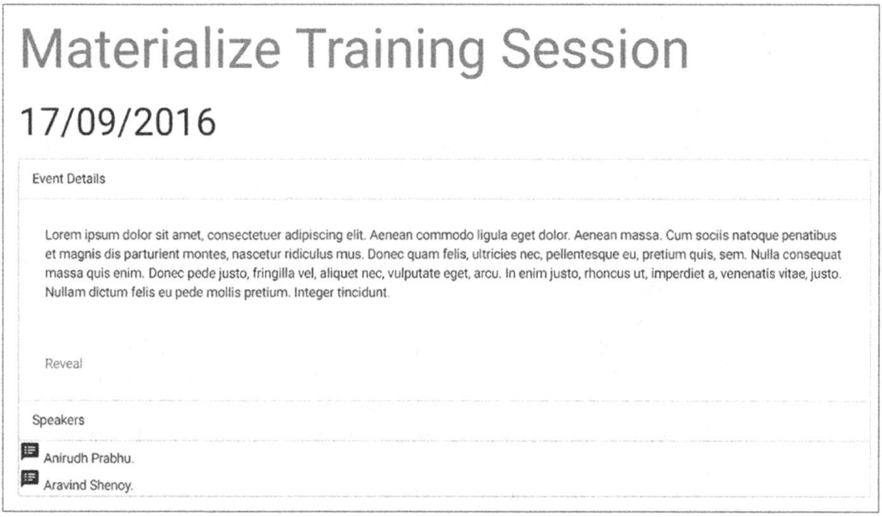

Materialize Training Session
17/09/2016

Event Details

Lorem ipsum dolor sit amet, consectetuer adipiscing elit. Aenean commodo ligula eget dolor. Aenean massa. Cum sociis natoque penatibus et magnis dis parturient montes, nascetur ridiculus mus. Donec quam felis, ultricies nec, pellentesque eu, pretium quis, sem. Nulla consequat massa quis enim. Donec pede justo, fringilla vel, aliquet nec, vulputate eget, arcu. In enim justo, rhoncus ut, imperdiet a, venenatis vitae, justo. Nullam dictum felis eu pede mollis pretium. Integer tincidunt.

Reveal

Speakers

Anirudh Prabhu.
Aravind Shenoy.

Figure 4-4. *Multiple panels open at once*

The default value for the data-collapsible attribute is accordion.

The collapsible usually doesn't need any JavaScript initialization. However, if you need to dynamically modify the elements or the behavior of the collapsible, then you need to use JavaScript.

To demonstrate this, you can add a link containing the words "Reveal Agenda". This link will add another collapsible content to the existing sets of collapsible content. Listing 4-5 shows the code for this example.

Listing 4-5. Using JavaScript

```
<!DOCTYPE html>
<html>
<head>
    <!--Import Google Icon Font-->
    <link href="http://fonts.googleapis.com/icon?family=Material+Icons"
    rel="stylesheet">
    <!--Import materialize.css-->
    <link type="text/css" rel="stylesheet" href="https://cdnjs.
    cloudflare.com/ajax/libs/materialize/0.97.7/css/materialize.min.
    css"  media="screen,projection"/>

    <!--Let browser know website is optimized for mobile-->
    <meta name="viewport" content="width=device-width, initial-scale=1.0"/>
    <style>

    </style>
</head>

<body style="padding:25px">
<!--Import jQuery before materialize.js-->
<script type="text/javascript" src="https://code.jquery.com/jquery-
2.1.1.min.js"></script>
<script type="text/javascript" src="https://cdnjs.cloudflare.com/ajax/libs/
materialize/0.97.7/js/materialize.min.js"></script>
<div class="row">
    <h1 class=" deep-orange-text darken-3">Materialize Training Session</h1>
    <h3>17/09/2016</h3>
    <ul class="collapsible" data-collapsible="expandable">
        <li>
            <div class="collapsible-header active">Event Details</div>
            <div class="collapsible-body"><p>Lorem ipsum dolor sit amet,
            consectetuer adipiscing elit. Aenean commodo ligula eget
            dolor. Aenean massa. Cum sociis natoque penatibus et magnis
            dis parturient montes, nascetur ridiculus mus. Donec quam
            felis, ultricies nec, pellentesque eu, pretium quis, sem.
            Nulla consequat massa quis enim. Donec pede justo, fringilla
            vel, aliquet nec, vulputate eget, arcu. In enim justo, rhoncus
            ut, imperdiet a, venenatis vitae, justo. Nullam dictum felis
```

```
            eu pede mollis pretium. Integer tincidunt.</p><p><a href="#"
            class="addCollapsible">Reveal Agenda</a></p></div>
        </li>
        <li>
            <div class="collapsible-header">Speakers</div>
            <div class="collapsible-body">
                <ul>
                li><i class="material-icons">speaker_notes</i> Anirudh
                Prabhu.</li>
                <li><i class="material-icons">speaker_notes</i> Aravind
                Shenoy.</li>
                </ul>
            </div>
        </li>
    </ul>

</div>
<script type="text/javascript">
    $(function () {
        $(document).on('click','.addCollapsible',function (e) {
            e.preventDefault();
            $("ul.collapsible").append('<li><div class="collapsible-
            header">Agenda</div><div class="collapsible-body"><p>Lorem ipsum
            dolor sit amet, consectetuer adipiscing elit. Aenean commodo
            ligula eget dolor. Aenean massa. Cum sociis natoque penatibus et
            magnis dis parturient montes, nascetur ridiculus mus. Donec quam
            felis, ultricies nec, pellentesque eu, pretium quis, sem. Nulla
            consequat massa quis enim. Donec pede justo, fringilla vel,
            aliquet nec, vulputate eget, arcu. In enim justo, rhoncus ut,
            imperdiet a, venenatis vitae, justo. Nullam dictum felis eu pede
            mollis pretium. Integer tincidunt.</p></div></li>');
            $('.collapsible').collapsible();
        })
    })
</script>
</body>
</html>
```

In Listing 4-5, you use JavaScript to dynamically add content, which contains the collapsible header and content, by using jQuery's append method, which basically adds the new content at the end of a specified target element, which is ul.collapsible in your case, on clicking the *Reveal Agenda* link. You then reinitialize the collapsible elements using the collapsible() method so that all collapsibles behave symmetrically. See Figure 4-5.

Materialize Training Session

17/09/2016

Event Details

Lorem ipsum dolor sit amet, consectetuer adipiscing elit. Aenean commodo ligula eget dolor. Aenean massa. Cum sociis natoque penatibus et magnis dis parturient montes, nascetur ridiculus mus. Donec quam felis, ultricies nec, pellentesque eu, pretium quis, sem. Nulla consequat massa quis enim. Donec pede justo, fringilla vel, aliquet nec, vulputate eget, arcu. In enim justo, rhoncus ut, imperdiet a, venenatis vitae, justo. Nullam dictum felis eu pede mollis pretium. Integer tincidunt.

Reveal Agenda

Speakers

Agenda

Lorem ipsum dolor sit amet, consectetuer adipiscing elit. Aenean commodo ligula eget dolor. Aenean massa. Cum sociis natoque penatibus et magnis dis parturient montes, nascetur ridiculus mus. Donec quam felis, ultricies nec, pellentesque eu, pretium quis, sem. Nulla consequat massa quis enim. Donec pede justo, fringilla vel, aliquet nec, vulputate eget, arcu. In enim justo, rhoncus ut, imperdiet a, venenatis vitae, justo. Nullam dictum felis eu pede mollis pretium. Integer tincidunt.

Figure 4-5. *Dynamically adding content*

In Figure 4-5, you can see that clicking the Reveal Agenda link will display the content in that section, along with the content in the Event Details accordion.

Toasts

Using the Toast property you can provide notifications and alerts to the user. This is definitely a better alternative to using the default alert provided by the browser. A toast, when fired, appears and stays on the screen for the amount of milliseconds specified in the code. See Listing 4-6.

Listing 4-6. Using a Toast

```
<div class="row">
    <h1 class=" deep-orange-text darken-3">Materialize Training Session</h1>
    <h3>17/09/2016</h3>
    <a class="btn" onclick="Materialize.toast('You have been registered',
    2000)">Attending Event</a>
</div>
```

In Listing 4-6, you define the content (i.e. *Materialize Training Sessions*) along with the date in the heading tags. Then you create a button called Attending Event to which you include the following code for the onclick attribute (i.e. Materialize.toast). Then you define the text and the time the notification should stay on the screen. In this example, you use the content for the notification as "You have been registered" and specify the time as 2000 milliseconds.

The output of the code is shown in Figure 4-6. Upon clicking the button, you can see the notification (*You have been registered*), which will disappear after the stipulated time.

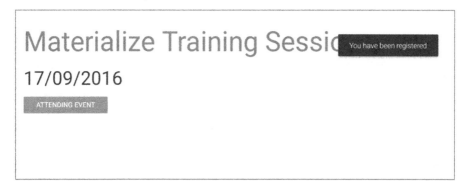

Figure 4-6. *A timed notification*

Remember that the content passed to the toast can be either standard text or can be HTML markup. For example, you can enclose the string you passed in the previous example in a <strong> tag, as shown in Listing 4-7.

Listing 4-7. Using a <strong> Tag

```
<div class="row">
    <h1 class=" deep-orange-text darken-3">Materialize Training Session</h1>
    <h3>17/09/2016</h3>
    <a class="btn" onclick="Materialize.toast('<strong>You have been
    registered</strong>', 2000)">Attending Event</a>
</div>
```

Also, you can use a pass callback function that can be executed once the toast disappears. You described the same in Listing 4-8; in it you use an alert function that will display *Thank you!* once the toast notification disappears.

Listing 4-8. A Thank You Message

```
<div class="row">
    <h1 class=" deep-orange-text darken-3">Materialize Training Session</h1>
    <h3>17/09/2016</h3>
    <a class="btn" onclick="Materialize.toast('<strong>You have been
    registered</strong>', 2000,'',function() {
      alert('Thank you!');
    })">Attending Event</a>
</div>
```

Figure 4-7 depicts the alert function that will be displayed after the toast notification goes off after 2000 milliseconds.

Figure 4-7. *Thank you!*

Finally, you can also use the rounded class to the notification so that the notification can have rounded edges. Implement the rounded class as the third parameter, as shown in Listing 4-9.

Listing 4-9. The rounded Class

```
<div class="row">
    <h1 class=" deep-orange-text darken-3">Materialize Training Session</h1>
    <h3>17/09/2016</h3>
    <a class="btn" onclick="Materialize.toast('<strong>You have been
    registered</strong>', 2000,'rounded')">Attending Event</a>
</div>
```

You can see the rounded notification in Figure 4-8.

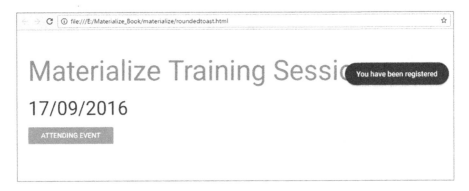

Figure 4-8. *A rounded notification*

You can choose another class instead of rounded for any specific result based on the parameter.

Tooltips

Tooltips are labels that are displayed upon hovering over an element. You can assign a tooltip to an element to give the end user information about that specific element.

Let's understand this using a simple example; see Listing 4-10.

Listing 4-10. A Tooltip

```
<a class="btn tooltipped" data-position="bottom" data-delay="50" data-
tooltip="Lorem ipsum dolor sit amet, consectetuer adipiscing elit. Aenean
commodo ligula eget dolor.">Teaser</a>
```

In this code, you create a button called Teaser and use the `tooltipped` class in conjunction with the `btn` class. Then you define the position of the tooltip to the bottom by assigning the `bottom` value to the `data-position` attribute and define a delay of 50 milliseconds.

This code produces the results shown in Figure 4-9.

Figure 4-9. *A tooltip*

No explicit JavaScript initialization is required if the tooltip elements have been present since the page load.

However, if the elements are to be added dynamically to the page, you need to initialize them for them to be fully functional. In Listing 4-11, you define the following:

- `Delay`: Amount of time by which the display of the tooltip is delayed.

- `Tooltip`: Text to be displayed inside the tooltip. This can be HTML markup too.

- `Position`: Direction for placement of the tooltip around the element.

- `Html`: A flag that indicates that the content passed is to be treated as HTML markup.

Listing 4-11. Dynamically Adding Elements

```
<!DOCTYPE html>
<html>
<head>
    <!--Import Google Icon Font-->
    <link href="http://fonts.googleapis.com/icon?family=Material+Icons"
    rel="stylesheet">
    <!--Import materialize.css-->
    <link type="text/css" rel="stylesheet" href="https://cdnjs.
    cloudflare.com/ajax/libs/materialize/0.97.7/css/materialize.min.
    css"  media="screen,projection"/>

    <!--Let browser know website is optimized for mobile-->
    <meta name="viewport" content="width=device-width, initial-scale=1.0"/>
</head>

<body style="padding:25px">
<!--Import jQuery before materialize.js-->
<script type="text/javascript" src="https://code.jquery.com/jquery-
2.1.1.min.js"></script>
<script type="text/javascript" src="https://cdnjs.cloudflare.com/ajax/libs/
materialize/0.97.7/js/materialize.min.js"></script>
<div class="row">
    <h1 class=" deep-orange-text darken-3">Materialize Training Session</h1>
    <h3>17/09/2016</h3>
    <a class="btn" data-position="bottom" data-delay="50" data-
    tooltip="Lorem ipsum dolor sit amet, consectetuer adipiscing elit.
    Aenean commodo ligula eget dolor.">Teaser</a>
</div>
<script type="text/javascript">
    $(function () {
        $(document).on("click",".btn",function(e){
            e.preventDefault()
            $(".row").append('<a class="btn tooltipped" data-
            position="bottom" data-delay="50" data-tooltip="Lorem ipsum
            dolor sit amet, consectetuer adipiscing elit. Aenean commodo
            ligula eget dolor.">Socials</a>');
            //Re-initialize the tooltip
            $('.tooltipped').tooltip();
        })
    })
</script>
</body>
</html>
```

In this example, you add click actions to the teaser button from your previous example. Upon clicking the button, another button (Socials) will be added to the page using the jQuery append property. Then you initialize the tooltip.

The output of Listing 4-11 is shown in Figure 4-10.

Figure 4-10. *Tooltips*

You can also introduce a parameter to the initialization function. For example, a delay of 50 seconds can be assigned as a parameter to the initialization of the tooltip, as showed in Listing 4-12.

Listing 4-12. Adding a Delay

```
$('.tooltipped').tooltip({delay:50});
```

Dropdown

Dropdowns are a handy utility for displaying information while clicking or hovering over an element. Listing 4-13 shows an example of the dropdown functionality.

Listing 4-13. Dropdown Functionality

```
<div class="row">
    <h1 class=" deep-orange-text darken-3">Materialize Training Session</h1>
    <h3>17/09/2016</h3>
    <!-- Dropdown Trigger -->
    <a class='dropdown-button btn' href='#' data-
     activates='countDropdown'>Number of attendees</a>

    <!-- Dropdown Structure -->
    <ul id='countDropdown' class='dropdown-content'>
        <li><a href="#!">one</a></li>
        <li><a href="#!">two</a></li>
        <li><a href="#!">three</a></li>
        <li><a href="#!">four</a></li>
    </ul>
</div>
```

In Listing 4-13, you add dropdowns for a specific button by using the dropdown-button class along with the btn class. Next, you use the data-activates attribute and assign a countDropdown as the value to it wherein the value will be used as an id with the <ul> list tag. In the <ul> tag, you also use the dropdown-content class.

The output of the code will display a button on the screen with the name *Number of attendees* as defined in the code. On clicking, the dropdown function is activated and you can see the four items as defined in the list. This is shown in Figure 4-11.

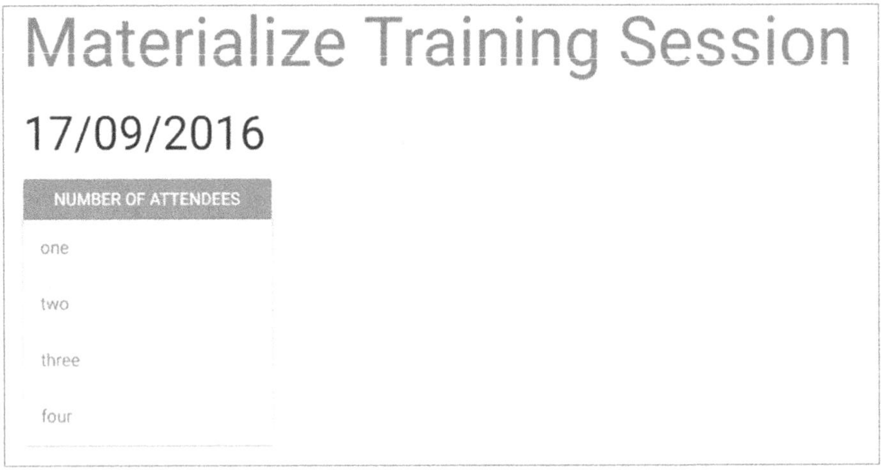

Figure 4-11. *A dropdown list*

You can also add dividers to separate options within the list. This can be done by defining the divider class to the specific list item defined by the <li> tag. Let's look at Listing 4-14 for an illustration.

Listing 4-14. Adding Dividers

```
<div class="row">
    <h1 class=" deep-orange-text darken-3">Materialize Training Session</h1>
    <h3>17/09/2016</h3>
    <!-- Dropdown Trigger -->
    <a class='dropdown-button btn' href='#' data-
    activates='countDropdown'>Number of attendees</a>

    <!-- Dropdown Structure -->
    <ul id='countDropdown' class='dropdown-content'>
        <li><a href="#!">one</a></li>
        <li><a href="#!">two</a></li>
        <li><a href="#!">three</a></li>
        <li><a href="#!">four</a></li>
        <li class="divider"></li>
```

```
        <li><a href="#!">Custom</a></li>
    </ul>
</div>
```

The output is shown in Figure 4-12.

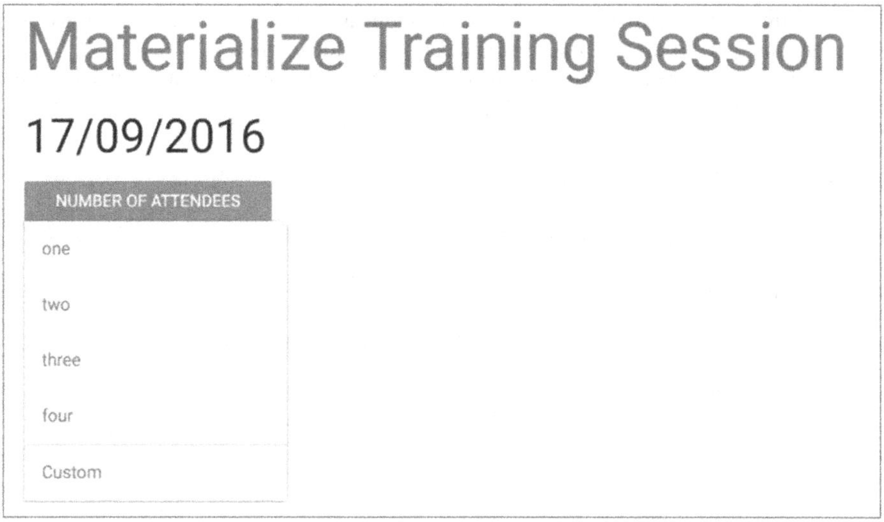

Figure 4-12. *Adding dividers*

In Figure 4-12, you can see that there is a dividing line before the Custom item in the list.

The following are the different data-attributes that can be used along with the Dropdown function:

- induration: Duration of the animation required for the dropdown to appear.

- outduration: Duration of the animation required for the dropdown to disappear.

- constrainwidth: With this option set to true (default), the width of the list will be same as the width of activating button.

- hover: With this option set to true, the dropdown will open on hovering over the activating button.

- gutter: This defines the spacing from edges.

- beloworigin: With this option set to true, the dropdown will appear below the activating button.

- stoppropagation: With this set to true, even bubbling will not occur on the dropdown activator button.

Some of these options are demonstrated in Listing 4-15.

Listing 4-15. Dropdown Options

```
<a class='dropdown-button btn' href='#' data-activates='countDropdown' data-
hover="true" data-beloworigin="true">Number of attendees</a>
```

In Listing 4-15, you use the data-hover attribute and set it to true, meaning hover is activated. You use the data-beloworigin and set the value to true.

As a result, on hovering, the dropdown is activated and the list is displayed below the button you hover on. This is shown in Figure 4-13.

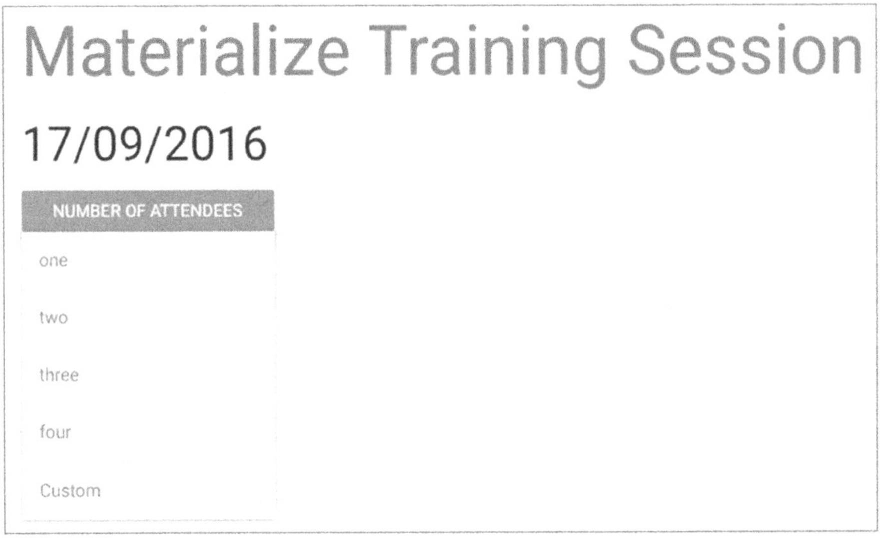

Materialize Training Session
17/09/2016

| NUMBER OF ATTENDEES |
| one |
| two |
| three |
| four |
| Custom |

Figure 4-13. *Dropdown options*

If the dropdown elements have been loaded since page load, you probably don't need the JavaScript explicitly. However, while adding the entire dropdown or part of it dynamically.

The options mentioned with the dropdown can be used in JavaScript initializations; however, there's a small change. You need to style the options in Camel case. For example, induration is used as induration but outduration becomes outDuration. See Listing 4-16.

Listing 4-16. Dropdown Options

```
<script type="text/javascript">
    $(function () {
        setTimeout(function () {
```

```
            $(".row").append(' <a class="dropdown-button btn"
            href="#" data-activates="countDropdown" data-hover="true"
            data-beloworigin="true">Number of attendees</a> <ul
            id="countDropdown" class="dropdown-content"><li><a
            href="#!">one</a></li><li><a href="#!">two</a></li><li><a
            href="#!">three</a></li><li><a href="#!">four</a></li><li
            class="divider"></li><li><a href="#!">Custom</a></li></ul>');
            $('.dropdown-button').dropdown({
                    hover: true,
                    belowOrigin: true
                }
            );
        },5000);
    })
</script>
```

In Listing 4-16, you use the setTimeout function of JavaScript to add the dropdown elements 5 seconds after the entire document is loaded. You use jQuery's append function to add the dropdown to the page. After appending the dropdown element, you initialize the dropdown using Materialize's dropdown function.

The output of the code is similar to the previous example. However, the dropdown has been added dynamically after the page load.

Modal

Modals help you overlay an element over your web site. A modal is generally used as an alternative to a conventional pop-up. You can see the information without leaving the page you are viewing. It also counts for awesome aesthetics and is a resourceful utility that significantly enhances usability.

In Materialize, to implement the Modal feature, you need a link that contains the id of the modal container in its href attribute. Unlike other JavaScript components, modals need to be initialized through JavaScript before they can be used.

Listing 4-17 shows the code snippet for the Modal feature.

Listing 4-17. The Modal Feature

```
<div class="row">
    <h1 class=" deep-orange-text darken-3">Materialize Training Session</h1>
    <h3>17/09/2016</h3>
    <a href="#TCModal" class="TCtrigger">Terms &amp; Condition</a>
    <div id="TCModal" class="modal">
        <div class="modal-content">
            <h4>Terms &amp; Conditions</h4>
            <p>Lorem ipsum dolor sit amet, consectetuer adipiscing elit.
Aenean commodo ligula eget dolor.....
</p>
        </div>
        <div class="modal-footer">
```

```
            <a href="#!" class=" modal-action modal-close waves-effect
            waves-green btn-flat">Agree</a>
        </div>
    </div>
</div>
<script type="text/javascript">
    $(document).ready(function(){
        $('.TCtrigger').leanModal();
    });
</script>
```

A modal structure consists of the `modal-content` and `modal-footer` classes. A `modal-content` is used to contain all the content that you wish to display when the modal opens. A `modal-footer` is a fixed area in the bottom, which is optional. A `modal-footer` is useful when you want to add buttons to the modal, as in this example where you have added the *Agree* button.

In Listing 4-17, you create a link called *Terms & Conditions*. Then, you set the value of the `href` attribute, which is the id of the following `<div>` to which you also assign the `modal` class. You then define another `<div>` within the preceding `<div>` to which you assign the `modal-content` class.

You create another `<div>` where you define the `modal-footer` class. `modal-footer` is needed for placing content in the footer, which stays in a fixed position regardless of the length of the content in the modal. After creating the necessary elements, you initialize the modal on the triggering element.

Clicking the Terms & Conditions link will open up a modal that contains the content for the Terms and Conditions as defined in the code. The output of clicking the Terms & Conditions link is shown in Figure 4-14.

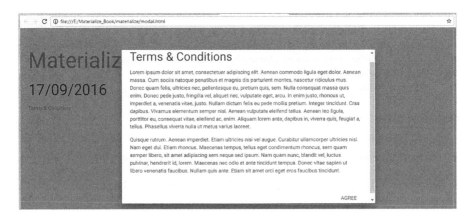

Figure 4-14. *The modal in action*

In Materialize, the modal can be customized using the following options:

- `dismissible`: Controls whether the modal can be closed by clicking the outer area.

- `opacity`: Controls the opacity of the modal background.

- `in_duration`: Controls the amount of time it takes for the modal to appear.

- `out_duration`: Controls the amount of time it takes for the modal to disappear.

- `ready`: A callback function that will execute the code inside it when the modal has opened up.

- `complete`: A callback function that will execute the code inside it when the modal has closed.

You can initialize a modal with options, as shown in Listing 4-18.

Listing 4-18. Modal Options

```
$('.TCtrigger').leanModal({
        opacity: .3,
        in_duration: 100,
        out_duration: 50
    });
```

Here you set the `opacity` to .3, `in_duration` to 100, and `out_duration` to 50.

In Materialize, modals cans be invoked programmatically through the code. This feature is quite handy when you intend to show the modal with some information without any user interaction. In Materialize, the methods available for this feature are `openModal` and `closeModal`.

Listing 4-19 shows how to use the `openModal` function. You can do the same with the `closeModal`.

Listing 4-19. The openModal Function

```
$('.TCtrigger').openModal()
```

ScrollFire

Materialize provides the ability to track how much an end user has scrolled on a long page and execute the assigned callback functions depending on that length. To implement this, you need to provide three parameters: an element that will be affected, the offset after which the specific callback is to be triggered, and the callback itself. You can pass these parameters for more than one offset. See Listing 4-20.

Listing 4-20. Tracking User Scrolling

```
<h1 class="currentPosition" style="position: fixed;top:
10px;left: 10px;width: 100%;height:300px">You have crossed:<span
class="progressCounter"></span>px </h1>
<div class="longDiv" style="height: 2000px;"></div>
<script type="text/javascript">
    $(document).ready(function(){
        var options = [
                    {selector: '.longDiv', offset: 500, callback:
                    function () {
                            $('.progressCounter').text(500).
                            css({"background":"#B00"});
                        }
                    },
                    {selector: '.longDiv', offset: 1000, callback:
                    function() {
                            $('.progressCounter').text(900).
                            css({"background":"#0B0"});
                        }
                    },
                    {selector: '.longDiv', offset: 1400, callback:
                    function() {
                            $('.progressCounter').text(1400).
                            css({"background":"#00B"});
                        }
                    }
        ];
        Materialize.scrollFire(options);
    });
</script>
```

A scrollFire configuration consists of three parameters:

1. selector: The element to be monitored for scrolling.

2. offset: The point within the scrollable limit where some
    action needs to be triggered.

3. callback: The action to be triggered on reaching a specific
    offset.

In Listing 4-20, you create a long <div> with a height of 2000px so that the page is
scrollable.

A ScrollFire monitors the element specified in the selector parameter as to how
much it has been scrolled. You then initialize Materialize's ScrollFire with configuration.
This configuration will tell how ScrollFire should behave when you scroll to a specific
length of the page. ScrollFire works only in one direction (from top to bottom) and only

one time. These actions won't be repeated by scrolling back and forth. Let's say that you have one of them monitoring for 900, which means that when the scrolling exceeds 900px from the top, a callback will be fired. In your example, you select the `ProgressCounter` span, change the textual content inside it to 900, and then change its background color to green. See the results in Figure 4-15 when the scroll offset crosses 900px.

Figure 4-15. *ScrollFire in action*

ScrollSpy

Web design increasingly uses ScrollSpy navigation. It allows the users to scroll to each section while they are on the same page. The menu is dependent on the scrolling position, which is highlighted to indicate to the users where they are currently.

Listing 4-21 shows the code for the ScrollSpy feature.

Listing 4-21. The ScrollSpy Feature

```
<div class="row">
    <h1 class=" deep-orange-text darken-3">Materialize Training Session</h1>
    <h3>17/09/2016</h3>
    <div class="col s12 m9 l10">
        <div id="eventDetails" class="section scrollspy">
            <h3>Event Details</h3>
            <p>Lorem ipsum dolor sit amet, consectetuer adipiscing elit.
            Aenean commodo ligula eget dolor...... .</p>
            <p>Lorem ipsum dolor sit amet, consectetuer adipiscing elit.
            Aenean commodo ligula eget dolor.......</p>
            <p>Lorem ipsum dolor sit amet, consectetuer adipiscing elit.
            Aenean commodo ligula eget dolor...... </p>
        </div>
        <div id="speakers" class="section scrollspy">
            <ul>
                <li><i class="material-icons">speaker_notes</i> Anirudh
                Prabhu.</li>
```

```
                    <li><i class="material-icons">speaker_notes</i> Aravind
                    Shenoy.</li>
                </ul>
            </div>
            <div id="eventOutline" class="section scrollspy">
                <h3>Event Outline</h3>
                <p>Lorem ipsum dolor sit amet, consectetuer adipiscing elit.
                Aenean commodo ligula eget dolor.....</p>
                <p>Lorem ipsum dolor sit amet, consectetuer adipiscing elit.
                Aenean commodo ligula eget dolor...... ..</p>
                <p>Lorem ipsum dolor sit amet, consectetuer adipiscing elit.
                Aenean commodo ligula eget dolor.......</p>
                <p>Lorem ipsum dolor sit amet, consectetuer adipiscing elit.
                Aenean commodo ligula eget dolor....... </p>
            </div>
        </div>
        <div class="col hide-on-small-only m3 l2">
            <div style="position: fixed">
            <ul class="section table-of-contents">
                <li><a href="#eventDetails">Event Details</a></li>
                <li><a href="#speakers">Speakers</a></li>
                <li><a href="#eventOutline">Event Outline</a></li>
            </ul>
            </div>
        </div>
    </div>
</div>
<script type="text/javascript">
    $(document).ready(function(){
        $('.scrollspy').scrollSpy();
    });
</script>
```

In Listing 4-21, you create two sections within the page. You define the col s12 m9 l10 class, meaning the content will span across 12 columns on the small screen, 9 columns on a medium screen, and 10 columns on a large screen. You define the content for Event Details within a <div> and assign an id and the section and scrollspy class to it. Similarly, you create two more <div>s and assign unique ids and the scrollspy class to them. After defining the content, you create a <div> where you define the scrollspy links within the <ul> and its <li> tags. Moving forward, you initialize the scrollspy at the end using the document.ready function.

The output of the code is shown in Figure 4-16.

Figure 4-16. *ScrollSpy in action*

As you can see, the links are highlighted while scrolling down the screen based on the content on the screen.

SideNav

SideNavs are slide-out menus that are usually implemented for navigation or show controls that need not be visible all the time. Listing 4-22 shows the code for the sideNav feature.

Listing 4-22. The SideNav Feature

```
<ul id="slide-out" class="side-nav">
    <li><a href="#!">Register</a></li>
    <li><a href="#!">More info</a></li>
</ul>
<a href="#" data-activates="slide-out" class="button-collapse show-on-
large"><i class="material-icons">menu</i></a>

<div class="row">
    <h1 class=" deep-orange-text darken-3">Materialize Training Session</h1>
    <h3>17/09/2016</h3>
<script type="text/javascript">
    $(function () {
        $(".button-collapse").sideNav();
    })
</script>
```

In Listing 4-22, you assign the side-nav class to the <ul> tag whereas the <li> tags within the <ul> tags are where you define the links. Then you create an anchor tag which will act as a trigger to display the sideNav. After the elements are in place, you use the sideNav() function of Materialize to initialize and make the sideNav functional on the click of the anchor.

Figure 4-17 depicts the menu, which slides in once the button is triggered.

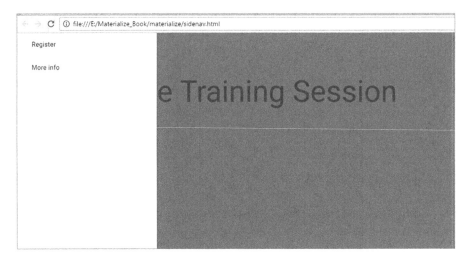

Figure 4-17. *The sideNav menu*

The sideNav can be further customized using the following options:

- `menuWidth`: Specifies the width of the slide-out menu.
- `edge`: Specifies from which edge of the browser the sideNav will appear.
- `closeOnClick`: Specifies whether the sideNav should close when its internal links are clicked.

An example of initializing with these options is shown in Listing 4-23.

Listing 4-23. SideNav Options

```
<script type="text/javascript">
    $(function () {
        $(".button-collapse").sideNav({
            menuWidth:200,
            edge: 'right',
            closeOnClick: true
        });
    })
</script>
```

Materialize also provides methods by which you can open or close sideNav programmatically using the code.

Listing 4-24 shows the code for the SideNav using the show and hide parameters, leading to displaying and hiding the SideNav content.

Listing 4-24. SideNav Parameters

```
// Show sideNav
  $('.button-collapse').sideNav('show');
  // Hide sideNav
  $('.button-collapse').sideNav('hide');
```

You can also have the SideNav visible by default without using any JavaScript code. Add a fixed class to the <ul> tag in conjunction with the side-nav class

Listing 4-25 shows the line of code that is required to enable the SideNav content to be visible on code execution.

Listing 4-25. Make SideNav Content Visible

```
<ul id="slide-out" class="side-nav fixed">
```

You can also specify the padding for the content area so that the SideNav won't overlay the content. Add the padding to the row class to enable the padding and define the style accordingly. Listing 4-26 shows the CSS markup to explain the same.

Listing 4-26. CSS: Adding Padding to the row Class

```
<style>
        .row {
            padding-left: 300px;
        }

        @media only screen and (max-width : 992px) {
            .row {
                padding-left: 0;
            }
        }
</style>
```

The output of the code is displayed in Figure 4-18.

Figure 4-18. SideNav Options

Tabs

Tabs are popular in web design to present content in a compact way. They allows you to keep multiple documents open in a single window. You can use tabs as a navigation widget to switch between content, resulting in a systematic and clean layout.

Listing 4-27 contains the code for the Tab feature.

Listing 4-27. The Tab Feature

```
<div class="row">
    <h1 class=" deep-orange-text darken-3">Materialize Training Session</h1>
    <h3>17/09/2016</h3>
    <div class="row">
        <div class="col s12">
            <ul class="tabs">
                <li class="tab col s3"><a href="#eventDetails"
                class="active">Event details</a></li>
                <li class="tab col s3"><a href="#speakers">Speakers</a></li>
                <li class="tab col s3"><a href="#eventOutline">Event
                Outline</a></li>
            </ul>
        </div>
        <div id="eventDetails" class="col s12">
            <h2>Event Details</h2>
            <p>Lorem ipsum dolor sit amet, consectetuer adipiscing elit.
            Aenean commodo ligula eget dolor.... </p>
        </div>
        <div id="speakers" class="col s12">
            <h2>Speakers</h2>
            <ul>
                <li><i class="material-icons">speaker_notes</i> Anirudh
                Prabhu.</li>
                <li><i class="material-icons">speaker_notes</i> Aravind
                Shenoy.</li>
            </ul>
        </div>
        <div id="eventOutline" class="col s12">
            <h2>Event Outline</h2>
            <p>Lorem ipsum dolor sit amet, consectetuer adipiscing elit.
            Aenean commodo ligula eget dolor....</p>
        </div>
    </div>
```

In Listing 4-27, you create a <div> class to which you assign the row class. Within that <div>, you create another <div> spanning across 12 columns. You create three tabs using the tabs class for the <ul> tag and tab class for each <li> tag spanning across three columns. After that, you close the ⟨ul⟩ tag and the ⟨div⟩ tag. You open a new ⟨div⟩ to host the content for the three tabs. You assign the id to the ⟨div⟩ class for the first tab wherein the id is the value of the href attribute for the previously defined ⟨li⟩ class. Similarly, you create two more ⟨div⟩s for the remaining two tabs and assign the ids for them, which are the value of the href attribute for the respective ⟨li⟩ tags.

The output is shown in Figure 4-19.

Figure 4-19. *Tabs in action*

Tabs do not require JavaScript initialization unless you add the tabs dynamically. Meanwhile, you can also disable a tab by adding the disabled class to the tab that you want to deactivate. Listing 4-28 shows the code for the disabled class and Figure 4-20 shows the results.

Listing 4-28. The disabled Class

```
<ul class="tabs">
                <li class="tab col s3"><a href="#eventDetails"
class="active">Event details</a></li>
                <li class="tab col s3"><a href="#speakers">Speakers</a></li>
                <li class="tab col s3 disabled"><a
                href="#eventOutline">Event Outline</a></li>
</ul>
```

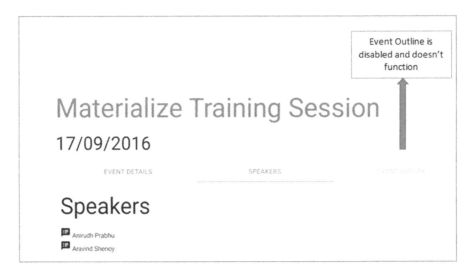

Figure 4-20. *The disabled class in action*

Also, you can make any tab active by default by adding the `active` class to the anchor within the ‹li› tag, as shown in Listing 4-28.

The default behavior of the tabs is to ignore the default behavior of the anchors inside it. However, you can override this behavior. To do so, add an URL to the `href` attribute of the anchor and an additional `target` attribute with a `_self` or `_blank` value. This is demonstrated in Listing 4-29.

Listing 4-29. Overriding Default Behavior

```
<ul class="tabs">
            <li class="tab col s3"><a href="#eventDetails"
            class="active">Event details</a></li>
            <li class="tab col s3"><a href="#speakers">Speakers</a></li>
            <li class="tab col s3"><a href="https://github.com/Dogfalo/
            materialize" target="_blank">Event Outline</a></li>
        </ul>
```

Upon executing the code, you will get the output shown in Figure 4-19. However, when you click the third tab (Event Outline), you will be directed to a different page, in this case, the Materialize Git Hub page, as depicted in Figure 4-21.

Figure 4-21. *Clicking tabs*

Materialize also provides methods by which you can select a tab programmatically. This can be done by the select_tab method, shown in Listing 4-30.

Listing 4-30. The secect_tab Method

```
$('ul.tabs').tabs('select_tab', 'speakers');
```

Materialize also provides an option to assign a callback, which will get executed every time a tab is changed. This is done by assigning a callback function to the onShow option; see Listing 4-31.

Listing 4-31. The onShow Option

```
<script type="text/javascript">
    $(document).ready(function(){
        $('ul.tabs').tabs({
            onShow:function (tab) {
                console.log(tab);
                alert("Tab changed")
            }
        });
    });
</script>
```

The output of the code is shown in Figure 4-19. However, when you click the second or third tab, you will receive an alert stating that the tab is changed, as depicted in Figure 4-22.

Figure 4-22. *The tab changed*

Waves

Materialize added an external library as part of its package that allows you to create an ink effect as part of the material design immersive feature.

To add a wave effect button, you simply need to add waves-effect to the button. If you want the wave effect to appear light (white), you need two classes: one that enables the wave effect and another for wave-color. So for a red wave effect, you add the classes shown in Listing 4-32.

Listing 4-32. Adding a Red Wave Effect

```
<a href="#!" class="waves-effect waves-red btn">Click me!</a>
```

You can see the results in Figure 4-23.

Figure 4-23. *Wave effect*

Click the Click Me button in the output and watch the wave effect wherein it creates a ripple effect of a red wave before it turns back to green.

Transitions

Materialize provides two built-in transitions that can be used as standalone features or along with its ScrollFire plug-in to add some jazz to the application. These two transitions are

- showStaggeredList

- fadeInImage

The first transition makes the contents of the list visible one by one, transitioning from left to right; see Listing 4-33.

Listing 4-33. The showStaggeredList Transition

```
<h1 class=" deep-orange-text darken-3">Materialize Training Session</h1>
<h3>17/09/2016</h3>
<a href="#!" class="waves-effect waves-light btn" onclick="Materialize.
showStaggeredList('.speakers')">Reveal the speakers</a>
<ul class="speakers">
    <li style="opacity: 0"><i class="material-icons">speaker_notes</i>
    Anirudh Prabhu.</li>
    <li style="opacity: 0"><i class="material-icons">speaker_notes</i>
    Aravind Shenoy.</li>
</ul>
```

In Listing 4-33, you use waves-effect for the button (Reveal the Speakers) to deliver an ink effect. Then you use an onclick action on the button and assign it the showStaggeredList function, followed by a list where you assign the speakers class to the <ul> tag. Remember that you use the speakers class in the showStaggeredList to link it with the list.

The output of the code is shown in Figure 4-24.

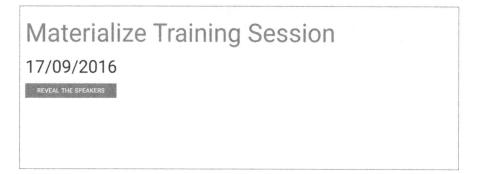

Figure 4-24. *The showStaggeredList effect at the start*

Remember that for the showStaggeredList to work, the list items need an opacity of 0.

In Figure 4-24, you click the Reveal the Speakers button to display a waves effect on the button while displaying the two speakers in conjunction with the material icons transitioning from left to right. This end result is shown in Figure 4-25.

Figure 4-25. *The end result*

The fadeInImage transition is used to fade in images with a unique animation of grayscales and brightness. In Listing 4-34, you set the opacity to 0 in order to show the fade effect. In the anchor link, you use the button displaying the waves effect and define the onclick property, which will result in a fade-in effect, like you used in the fadeInImage property. The class surpriseImage is assigned to the <img> tag wherein the class is the same called by the onclick function.

Listing 4-34. Setting the Opacity to 0

```
<h1 class=" deep-orange-text darken-3">Materialize Training Session</h1>
<h3>17/09/2016</h3>
<a href="#!" class="waves-effect waves-light btn" onclick="Materialize.
fadeInImage('.surpriseImage')">Reveal the Picture</a>
<img src="images/sample.jpg" style="opacity: 0;display: block;"
class="surpriseImage">
```

The output of the code is shown in Figure 4-26.

Materialize Training Session
17/09/2016
REVEAL THE PICTURE

Figure 4-26. *Reveal the picture*

When you click on the Reveal the Picture button, there is a waves effect on the button and below the button. The image displays a fade-in transition effect; see Figure 4-27.

Figure 4-27. *Ta-da!*

Carousel

Materialize provides a versatile carousel component that is fully responsive, scales with the container box, and offers touch and swipe support. A basic example of a carousel is demonstrated in Listing 4-35.

Listing 4-35. A Carousel

```
<h1 class=" deep-orange-text darken-3">Image Gallery</h1>
<div class="carousel">
    <a class="carousel-item" href="#one!"><img src="images/bg1.jpg"></a>
    <a class="carousel-item" href="#two!"><img src="images/bg2.jpg"></a>
    <a class="carousel-item" href="#three!"><img src="images/bg3.jpg"></a>
</div>
<script type="text/javascript">
    $(document).ready(function(){
        $('.carousel').carousel();
    });
</script>
```

Initially, you create a `<div>` with the `carousel` class. Then you enclose the `carousel-item` class to each link for each `<a>` tag. Then you initialize the JavaScript for the carousel, which will result in the output in Figure 4-28.

Figure 4-28. *A carousel of images*

Materialize allows you to customize the carousel by providing the options listed here:

- `time_constant`: Time taken for the movement of the image.

- `dist`: This is the perspective zoom, which gives a feel of the depth by varying the size of image.

- `shift`: This sets the spacing for the image in the center.

- `padding`: This sets the padding between the items that are not in the center.

- `Full_width`: This displays the images at their full width.

- `Indicators`: This sets the indicators shown along with the carousel.

- `No_wrap`: This says that the carousel should not keep looping.

Listing 4-36 shows the use of some of the preceding carousel properties. You add the `carousel-slider` class in conjunction with the `carousel` class for the `<div>` tag. Then you define the `width` of the carousel. Then you initialize the JavaScript for the carousel and set the full `width` to `true`.

Listing 4-36. Carousel Options

```
<h1 class=" deep-orange-text darken-3">Image Gallery</h1>
<div class="carousel carousel-slider" style="width: 720px;">
    <a class="carousel-item" href="#one!"><img src="images/bg1.jpg"></a>
```

```
    <a class="carousel-item" href="#two!"><img src="images/bg2.jpg"></a>
    <a class="carousel-item" href="#three!"><img src="images/bg3.jpg"></a>
</div>
<script type="text/javascript">
    $(document).ready(function(){
        $('.carousel.carousel-slider').carousel({full_width: true});
    });
</script>
```

The output of the code is shown in Figure 4-29.

Figure 4-29. *Carousel options*

Carousel doesn't restrict itself to images but also supports content. Listing 4-37 contains an example.

Listing 4-37. Carousel Content

```
<h1 class=" deep-orange-text darken-3">Content Gallery</h1>
<div class="carousel carousel-slider center" data-indicators="true"
style="width: 720px;">
    <div class="carousel-item red white-text" href="#one!">
        <h2>First Panel</h2>
        <p class="white-text">Lorem ipsum dolor sit amet, consectetuer
        adipiscing elit. Aenean commodo ligula eget dolor.... .</p>
    </div>
    <div class="carousel-item amber white-text" href="#two!">
```

```
    <h2>Second Panel</h2>
    <p class="white-text">Sed ut perspiciatis unde omnis iste natus
    error sit voluptatem accusantium doloremque laudantium, totam rem
    aperiam, eaque ipsa quae ab illo inventore... .</p>
</div>
<div class="carousel-item green white-text" href="#three!">
    <h2>Third Panel</h2>
    <p class="white-text">The European languages are members of the same
    family. Their separate existence is a myth. For science, music,
    sport, etc, Europe uses the same vocabulary... </p>
</div>
<div class="carousel-item blue white-text" href="#four!">
    <h2>Fourth Panel</h2>
    <p class="white-text">Far far away, behind the word mountains, far
    from the countries Vokalia and Consonantia, there live the blind
    texts. Separated they live in Bookmarksgrove right at the coast of
    the Semantics, a large language ocean... </p>
</div>
</div>
<script type="text/javascript">
    $(document).ready(function(){
        $('.carousel.carousel-slider').carousel({full_width: true});
    });
</script>
```

You used similar code in the earlier carousel code examples. However, here you add the data-indicators property to the <div> element with the carousel class and set it to true. Then you define the different carousel content and assign different colors to it, such as red, amber, green, and blue, in addition to defining the text as white.

Finally, you initialize the JavaScript for the carousel similar to the previous examples. You set the full width to true. Remember that you defined the carousel container width to 720px in the <div> with the carousel class.

The output of this code is shown in Figure 4-30.

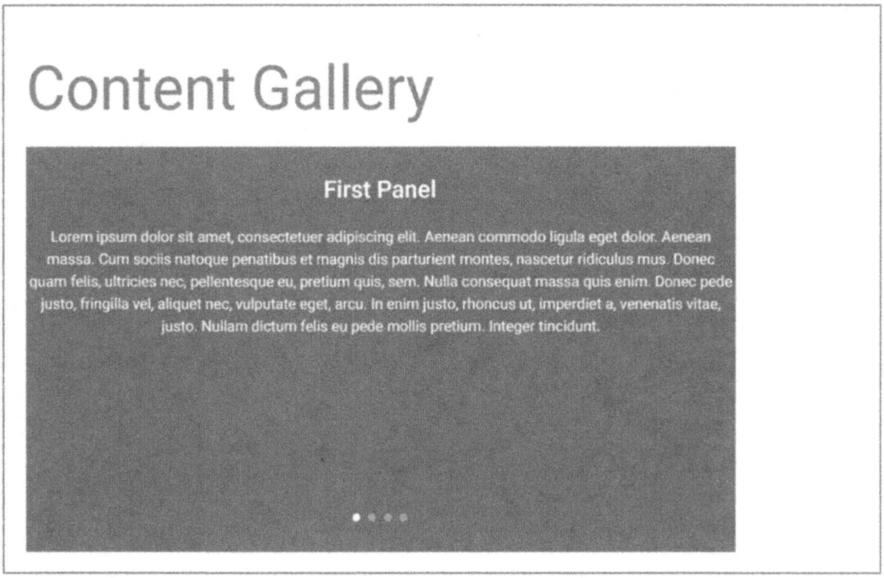

Content Gallery

First Panel

Lorem ipsum dolor sit amet, consectetuer adipiscing elit. Aenean commodo ligula eget dolor. Aenean massa. Cum sociis natoque penatibus et magnis dis parturient montes, nascetur ridiculus mus. Donec quam felis, ultricies nec, pellentesque eu, pretium quis, sem. Nulla consequat massa quis enim. Donec pede justo, fringilla vel, aliquet nec, vulputate eget, arcu. In enim justo, rhoncus ut, imperdiet a, venenatis vitae, justo. Nullam dictum felis eu pede mollis pretium. Integer tincidunt.

Figure 4-30. *Carousel Content*

Summary

In this chapter, you learned about the JavaScript-powered components of Materialize. You covered the self-initializing components like collapsible, waves, tooltip, etc. You also learned about components that require explicit initialization like tabs, carousel, toast, etc. You saw how to dynamically add content to these functions or how to customize them with various options.

You also viewed the carousel-based component provided by Materialize, which can be used for both images and content. You also covered how to add components on the fly and initialize them.

In next chapter, you will learn about components that are a blend of CSS and JavaScript, such as badges, cards, collections, etc.

Materialize Components

In the last chapter, you looked at the JavaScript-powered components in Materialize. In this chapter, you will touch base with the components that are a blend of JavaScript and CSS.

The very reason for using a CSS framework is to use its built-in user interface components. With its fantastic grid system and components, it is fairly easy to develop intricate web sites. In this chapter, you will take a look at various CSS components in Materialize.

The following are the topics you will learn about in an easy-to-understand manner:

- Badges
- Buttons
- Breadcrumbs
- Cards
- Chips
- Collections
- Footers
- Forms

Badges

A badge is a component used in conjunction with other components to indicate that there is an update to that component. Badges are most commonly used with components such as navbars and dropdowns, especially to show a number of unread items.

© Anirudh Prabhu and Aravind Shenoy 2016
A. Prabhu and A. Shenoy, *Introducing Materialize*, DOI 10.1007/978-1-4842-2349-9_5

Listing 5-1 shows the usage of badges in Materialize.

Listing 5-1. Badges

```
<!DOCTYPE html>
<html>
<head>
    <!--Import Google Icon Font-->
    <link href="http://fonts.googleapis.com/icon?family=Material+Icons"
    rel="stylesheet">
    <!--Import materialize.css-->
    <link type="text/css" rel="stylesheet" href="https://cdnjs.
    cloudflare.com/ajax/libs/materialize/0.97.7/css/materialize.min.
    css"  media="screen,projection"/>

    <!--Let browser know website is optimized for mobile-->
    <meta name="viewport" content="width=device-width, initial-scale=1.0"/>
</head>
<body style="padding:25px">
<!--Import jQuery before materialize.js-->
<script type="text/javascript" src="https://code.jquery.com/jquery-
2.1.1.min.js"></script>
<script type="text/javascript" src="https://cdnjs.cloudflare.com/ajax/libs/
materialize/0.97.7/js/materialize.min.js"></script>
<h1 class=" deep-orange-text darken-3">Materialize Training Session</h1>
<h3>Discussion</h3>
<div class="collection">
    <a href="#!" class="collection-item"><span class="title">How were the
    sessions?</span><span class="badge">302</span></a>
    <a href="#!" class="collection-item">Example files of session<span
    class="new badge">4</span></a>
    <a href="#!" class="collection-item">Reference material for
    framework</a>
    <a href="#!" class="collection-item">Photos<span class="badge">14</
    span></a>
</div>
</body>
</html>
```

In Listing 5-1, you create a <div> and assign a class called collection to it. Then you create a Discussion page. You create four links to list all the discussion topics in the collections section. You apply the class badge to three of the listed items. You define the badge class to two of them and a new badge for one of them. The listed items where you just used the badge class show the badge number next to their discussion topic. However, to make one of the badges to stand out, you use the new badge class for the "Example files of session" topic.

The output is depicted in Figure 5-1.

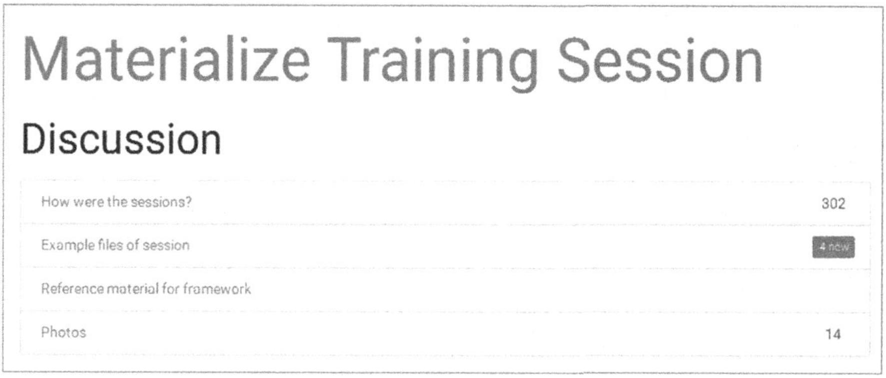

Materialize Training Session

Discussion

How were the sessions?	302
Example files of session	4 new
Reference material for framework	
Photos	14

Figure 5-1. *Badges*

Badges can also be used in dropdowns. Listing 5-2 demonstrates the code snippet wherein you create a page for downloading training material that has dropdowns. You assign the badge class to the first two list items within an inline <span> tag.

You use the dropdown-content class in the <ul> tag; the first item has an inline badge class whereas the second list item is assigned the new badge class. You create a button wherein you assign the dropdown button to the anchor tag's data-activates attribute. You then assign the id of the <ul> tag to the data-activates attribute.

Listing 5-2. Badges and Dropdowns

```
<h1 class=" deep-orange-text darken-3">Materialize Training Session</h1>
<h3>Training Material</h3>
<ul id="dropdown2" class="dropdown-content">
    <li><a href="#!">Ebooks<span class="badge">3</span></a></li>
    <li><a href="#!">Videos<span class="new badge">15</span></a></li>
    <li><a href="#!">Paperback</a></li>
</ul>
<a class="btn dropdown-button" href="#!" data-
activates="dropdown2">Download<i class="mdi-navigation-arrow-drop-down
right"></i></a>
```

This code results in a Download button which, upon being clicked, will show a dropdown menu with the badge for the first item (Ebooks) and new badge for the second item (Videos); see Figure 5-2.

89

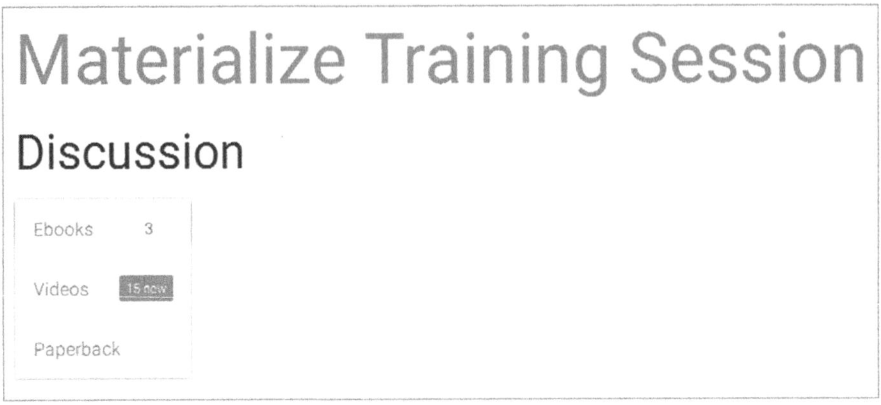

Materialize Training Session

Discussion

Ebooks   3

Videos   15 new

Paperback

Figure 5-2. Badges and dropdowns

Next, you will use the navbar feature and the dropdown options. Listing 5-3 depicts the usage of the badges in the Navbar feature.

You create a `<nav>` tag and assign the transparent `black-text` class to it. You create a `<div>` tag and assign the `nav-wrapper` class to it, followed by a list wherein you assign the `nav-mobile` id to it. You also assign the right class to the `<ul>` class in conjunction with the `hide-on-med-and-down` class. The `right` class will result in aligning your links to the right whereas the `hide-on-med-and-down` class will hide the navbar links on a medium and small screen. In the list items (`<li>` items within `<ul>`), you assign the deep-orange-text darken-3 class to define the color for them. Close the `<div>` and create the `<h1>` and `<h3>` tags to depict the page headings.

Listing 5-3. Navbar Options

```
<nav class="transparent black-text" style="box-shadow: initial">
    <div class="nav-wrapper">
        <ul id="nav-mobile" class="right hide-on-med-and-down">
            <li><a href="#!" class="deep-orange-text darken-3">Ebooks<span
            class="badge">3</span></a></li>
            <li><a href="#!" class="deep-orange-text darken-3">Videos<span
            class="new badge">15</span></a></li>
            <li><a href="#!" class="deep-orange-text darken-3">Paperback</
            a></li>
        </ul>
    </div>
</nav>
<h1 class="deep-orange-text darken-3">Materialize Training Session</h1>
<h3>Training Material</h3>
```

The output of the code is depicted in Figure 5-3.

Ebooks 3   Videos 19 new   Paperback

Materialize Training Session

Training Material

Figure 5-3. *Navbar options*

Buttons

Buttons are the most standard components used across web pages in web design. The more popular usage is in submission of forms and invoking actions.

Material design has three types of buttons:

- Standard buttons

- Fixed action button

- Flat buttons

Standard buttons are used commonly across web sites. In Materialize, you can create a standard button in Materialize using the btn class. You can also use the waves-effect along with assigning a color to enhance the animation effect.

You can also add icons within a button. Listing 5-4 shows the usage of buttons with built-in icons.

Listing 5-4. Buttons and Built-In Icons

```
<a class="btn">Standard Button</a>
<a class="waves-effect waves-light btn">Standard Button with wave</a>
<a class="waves-effect waves-light btn"><i class="material-icons
left">settings</i>Standard Button with icon</a>
<a class="waves-effect waves-light btn"><i class="material-icons
right">settings</i>Standard Button with icon</a>
```

In Listing 5-4, you create four buttons using the .btn class. In the last two buttons, you also assign the waves effect along with ingrained icons within the buttons. You use the material-icons class to the last two buttons and add the left and right to the material-icons class to place the icons to the left and right on the button, respectively.

The output of this listing is shown in Figure 5-4.

STANDARD BUTTON   STANDARD BUTTON WITH WAVE   ✿ STANDARD BUTTON WITH ICON   STANDARD BUTTON WITH ICON ✿

Figure 5-4. *Four buttons*

In Gmail, you can see a fixed action button at the right bottom corner. This button floats over content and can appear anywhere on the screen. This button will reveal additional controls under it when you hover over it.

Listing 5-5 shows the usage of the fixed action button.

Listing 5-5. The Fixed Action Button

```
<div class="fixed-action-btn" style="bottom: 45px; right: 24px;">
    <a class="btn-floating btn-large red">
        <i class="large material-icons">live_help</i>
    </a>
    <ul>
        <li><a class="btn-floating red"><i class="material-icons">email</
        i></a></li>
        <li><a class="btn-floating yellow darken-1"><i class="material-
        icons">chat</i></a></li>
        <li><a class="btn-floating green"><i class="material-icons">forum</
        i></a></li>
    </ul>
</div>
```

In Listing 5-5, you create a `<div>` class and assigned the `fixed-action-btn` class. Then you define the floating button using an anchor link to which you have defined `btn-floating` and `btn-large` red classes. Remember that the main button will always be used in an anchor tag. Then you create the hidden buttons using the list class (the `<ul>` and `<li>` tags under it). These hidden buttons are given the red, yellow, and green colors apart from using the `btn-floating` class. You also use the ingrained icons in those buttons such as e-mail, chat, and forums.

This results in a floating red button which, on hover, will display the three hidden buttons for e-mail, chat, and forums, as shown in Figure 5-5.

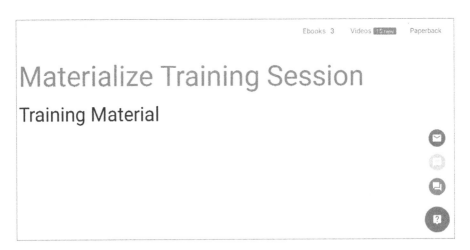

Figure 5-5. *Hidden buttons revealed*

The fixed action button revealed the hidden buttons vertically in the previous example. The buttons can also be displayed horizontally with a simple addition of the horizontal class to the <div> tag with the fixed-action-btn class. Listing 5-6 contains the code for the horizontal alignment of the controls.

Listing 5-6. Horizontal Alignment

```
<div class="fixed-action-btn horizontal" style="bottom: 45px; right: 24px;">
    <a class="btn-floating btn-large red">
        <i class="large material-icons">live_help</i>
    </a>
    <ul>
        <li><a class="btn-floating red"><i class="material-icons">email</
        i></a></li>
        <li><a class="btn-floating yellow darken-1"><i class="material-
        icons">chat</i></a></li>
        <li><a class="btn-floating green"><i class="material-icons">forum</
        i></a></li>
    </ul>
</div>
```

The output of this code will result in the floating button being displayed horizontally to the left, as depicted in Figure 5-6.

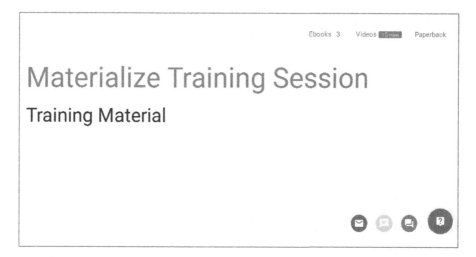

Figure 5-6. *Buttons are now horizontally aligned*

The default behavior of the fixed action button is to reveal the hidden options on hovering. However, you can change this behavior to a click action by simply adding a click-to-toggle class to the previous example. Listing 5-7 contains the code.

Listing 5-7. A Click Action

```
<div class="fixed-action-btn horizontal click-to-toggle" style="bottom:
45px; right: 24px;">
    <a class="btn-floating btn-large red">
        <i class="large material-icons">live_help</i>
    </a>
    <ul>
        <li><a class="btn-floating red"><i class="material-icons">email</
        i></a></li>
        <li><a class="btn-floating yellow darken-1"><i class="material-
        icons">chat</i></a></li>
        <li><a class="btn-floating green"><i class="material-icons">forum</
        i></a></li>
    </ul>
</div>
```

The output of the code will result in a floating button. However, on hover, there is no response but on clicking, the hidden control buttons are revealed as depicted in Figure 5-7.

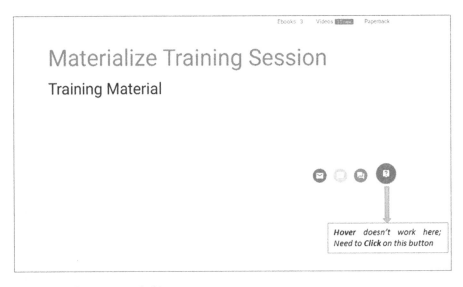

Figure 5-7. *Buttons revealed in a new way*

Now let's look at using flat buttons. Flat buttons do not have the shadows or colors associated with standard buttons. They are widely used in cards or modal components to avoid overlapping shadows while designing real-time web sites. The buttons appear like plain text in the normal state and will change their color on hover without any shadows or effects. Listing 5-8 shows how to use flat buttons.

Listing 5-8. Flat Buttons

```
<a class="btn">Standard Button</a>
<a class="waves-effect waves-light btn"><i class="material-icons
left">settings</i>Standard Button with icon</a>
<a class="waves-effect waves-teal btn-flat">Flat Button</a>
```

In Listing 5-8, you have three buttons: a standard button, a standard button with an icon, and a flat button.

This code results in three buttons. The last button is a flat button; when you hover over it, it changes its color without any shadows or effects, as in Figure 5-8.

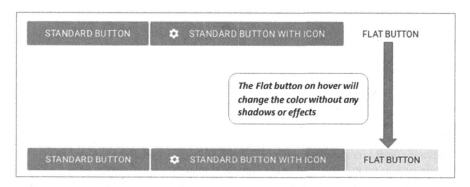

Figure 5-8. *Button types*

You can also create large buttons in Materialize by adding the `btn-large` class to the button.

Listing 5-9 shows the `btn-large` class assigned to the first button.

Listing 5-9. A Large Button

```
<a class="waves-effect waves-light btn-large">Large Button</a>
<a class="waves-effect waves-light btn">Normal Button</a>
```

See the result in Figure 5-9.

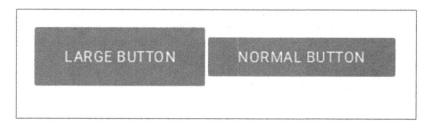

Figure 5-9. *A large button*

You can also disable the button by adding the disabled class to it. See Listing 5-10.

Listing 5-10. Disabling the Button

```
<a class="waves-effect waves-light btn-large disabled">Large Button</a>
<a class="waves-effect waves-light btn disabled">Normal Button</a>
```

In the code, you have defined the disabled class to the buttons. See Figure 5-10.

Figure 5-10. *A disabled button*

Cards

Cards are a flexible content container with a header and a footer and a wide range of content such as photos, text, and links. They are similar to panels from the early days of CSS web design. Depending on the type and length of the content, the supported actions in cards may vary accordingly.

See Listing 5-11 for an example of a card.

Listing 5-11. A Card

```
<div class="row">
    <div class="row">
        <div class="col s12 m6">
            <div class="card teal darken-4">
                <div class="card-content white-text">
                    <span class="card-title">Basic Card</span>
                    <p>Lorem ipsum dolor sit amet, consectetuer adipiscing
                    elit. Aenean commodo ligula eget dolor. Aenean massa.
                    Cum sociis natoque penatibus et magnis dis parturient
                    montes, nascetur ridiculus mus. Donec quam felis,
                    ultricies nec, pellentesque eu, pretium quis, sem. Nulla
                    consequat massa quis enim.</p>
                </div>
                <div class="card-action">
                    <a href="#">Action button</a>
                </div>
            </div>
        </div>
    </div>
</div>
```

A card consists of two sections: card content and `card-action`. A title can be added to the card using the `card-title` class. In Listing 5-11, you define a `<div>` element wherein you define the `card` class and add an inline span with the `card-title` class to it. Then you create an action button within another `<div>` using the `card-action` class.

Figure 5-11 depicts the output of the executed code.

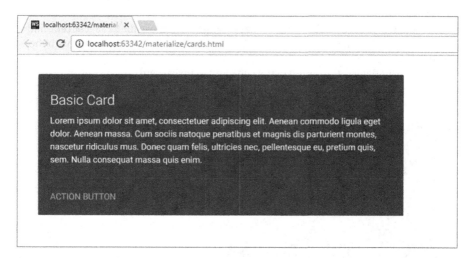

Figure 5-11. *A card*

Images can be used in the card. An image card is similar to a standard card with a thumbnail image inside it. See Listing 5-12.

Listing 5-12. An Image Card

```
<div class="row">
    <div class="row">
        <div class="col s12 m6">
            <div class="card teal darken-4">
                <div class="card-image">
                    <img src="images/bg1.jpg">
                    <span class="card-title">Basic Card</span>
                </div>
                <div class="card-content white-text">
                    <p>Lorem ipsum dolor sit amet, consectetuer adipiscing
                    elit. Aenean commodo ligula eget dolor. Aenean massa.
                    Cum sociis natoque penatibus et magnis dis parturient
                    montes, nascetur ridiculus mus. Donec quam felis,
                    ultricies nec, pellentesque eu, pretium quis, sem. Nulla
                    consequat massa quis enim.</p>
                </div>
                <div class="card-action">
```

97

```
                <a href="#">Action button</a>
            </div>
        </div>
    </div>
  </div>
</div>
```

All you did was add a `<div>` with the `card-image` class above the `card-content` and place an image using the `<img>` tag followed by an inline `<span>` element along with the card title.

Figure 5-12 depicts the output of the code for the image card.

Figure 5-12. *An image in a card*

You can also place the content of the card horizontally by adding the `horizontal` class to the `<div>` with the `card` class assigned to it. Listing 5-13 shows the code for this.

Listing 5-13. Horizontal Card Layout

```
<div class="row">
    <div class="row">
        <div class="col s12 m6">
            <div class="card horizontal teal darken-4">
                <div class="card-image">
                    <img src="images/sample.jpg">
                </div>
                <div class="card-stacked">
                <div class="card-content white-text">
```

```
        <span class="card-title">Basic Card</span>
        <p>Lorem ipsum dolor sit amet, consectetuer adipiscing
        elit. Aenean commodo ligula eget dolor. Aenean massa.
        Cum sociis natoque penatibus et magnis dis parturient
        montes, nascetur ridiculus mus. Donec quam felis,
        ultricies nec, pellentesque eu, pretium quis, sem. Nulla
        consequat massa quis enim.</p>
      </div>
      <div class="card-action">
        <a href="#">Action button</a>
      </div>
    </div>
  </div>
 </div>
</div>
```

In this code, you assign the horizontal class to the <div> with the card class. Also,
you wrap the <div> containing the card-content class and the other <div> containing
the card-action class within a parent <div> to which you assign the card-stacked class.
See Figure 5-13 for the result.

Figure 5-13. Another card layout

99

Until now, you have seen cards where the information is displayed at once. Another variant is where you show the information upon user activation. All you need to do is add another <div> with the classes card-reveal and activator to the element that will reveal the hidden content.

Listing 5-14 depicts an example of a card wherein the information is displayed on user action.

Listing 5-14. User Action

```
<div class="row">
    <div class="row">
        <div class="col s12 m6">
            <div class="card teal darken-4 sticky-action">
                <div class="card-image">
                    <img src="images/bg1.jpg">
                    <span class="card-title activator" style="width:
                    100%">Basic Card<i class="material-icons right">more_
                    vert</i></span>
                </div>
                <div class="card-content white-text">
                    <p>Lorem ipsum dolor sit amet, consectetuer adipiscing
                    elit. Aenean commodo ligula eget dolor. Aenean massa.
                    Cum sociis natoque penatibus et magnis dis parturient
                    montes, nascetur ridiculus mus. Donec quam felis,
                    ultricies nec, pellentesque eu, pretium quis, sem. Nulla
                    consequat massa quis enim.</p>
                </div>
                <div class="card-reveal">
                    <span class="card-title grey-text text-darken-
                    4">Detailed information<i class="material-icons
                    right">close</i></span>
                    <p>Here is some more information about this product that
                    is revealed once clicked on.</p>
                </div>
                <div class="card-action">
                    <a href="#">Action button</a>
                </div>
            </div>

        </div>
    </div>
</div>
```

In this code snippet, you add the activator class to the <span> tag alongside the card-title class. You then add the card-reveal class to a <div> element where you define the content that is revealed upon clicking the activator material icon.

The output of the code is shown in Figure 5-14.

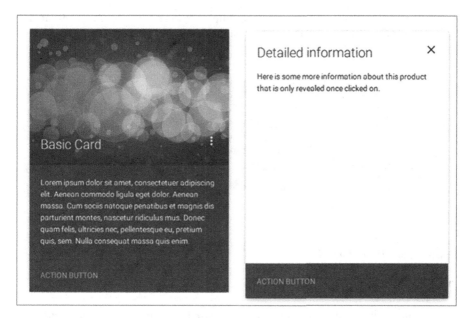

Figure 5-14. *User Actions*

From Figure 5-14, you can see that clicking the icon in the Basic Card image reveals the Detailed information section. Also, you can also see that you can close and run the action again and again. That is because you used the `sticky-action` to the `<div>` containing the card class. The `sticky-action` class makes the card action visible when it is added to the complete card. This is useful when you don't use the `sticky-action` class; it covers the card when the information is revealed.

Finally, if you need the card to only display information, you can always go old school by using the `card-panel` class. This results in an output without actions or titles. See Listing 5-15 contains the code snippet for the card panel feature.

Listing 5-15. The Card Panel

```
<div class="row">
        <div class="col s12 m6">
            <div class="card-panel teal">
          <span class="white-text">
            Lorem ipsum dolor sit amet, consectetuer adipiscing elit.
            Aenean commodo ligula eget dolor. Aenean massa. Cum sociis
            natoque penatibus et magnis dis parturient montes, nascetur
            ridiculus mus. Donec quam felis, ultricies nec, pellentesque
            eu, pretium quis, sem. Nulla consequat massa quis enim
        </span>
    </div>
</div>
```

In Listing 5-15, the structure looks quite simple: all you do is assign the `card-panel` class to the `<div>` within which the content using the inline `<span>` tag. See Figure 5-15.

> Lorem ipsum dolor sit amet, consectetuer adipiscing
> elit. Aenean commodo ligula eget dolor. Aenean
> massa. Cum sociis natoque penatibus et magnis dis
> parturient montes, nascetur ridiculus mus. Donec
> quam felis, ultricies nec, pellentesque eu, pretium quis,
> sem. Nulla consequat massa quis enim

Figure 5-15. *The card panel*

Chips

A chip is an excellent utility wherein the capsule-based structure can be used for little bits of information. It is quite handy in mobile applications where you need to display tags. You must have seen the contacts that are capsule-shaped when you add contacts to the "To" field in e-mails.

Chips can be used with or without JavaScript. Listing 5-16 demonstrates the Chips utility without JavaScript.

Listing 5-16. The Chips Utility without JavaScript

```
<div class="row" style="margin-top: 10px;margin-left: 10px">
    <span class="chip"><img src="images/img1.jpg"> Jim Morrison </span>
    <span class="chip"><img src="images/img2.png"> Jimi Hendrix </span>
    <span class="chip"><img src="images/img3.png"> Freddie Mercury </span>
</div>
```

In this code, you used the `<div>` element and added the `row` class. Within the parent `<div>`, you use three inline `<span>` tags and define the images of the rockstars (namely Jim Morrison, Jimi Hendrix, and Freddie Mercury) inside it.

Figure 5-16 depicts the capsules created due to the Chips feature.

Figure 5-16. *Rockstar capsules*

You can also allocate a close icon for each chip to enable users to remove the created chip. You add a a close class using the built-in material icons for each span element inside the <div> element. See Listing 5-17.

Listing 5-17. The Close Icon and Class

```
<div class="row" style="margin-top: 10px;margin-left: 10px">
    <span class="chip"><img src="images/img1.jpg"> Jim Morrison <i
    class="close material-icons">close</i></span>
    <span class="chip"><img src="images/img2.png"> Jimi Hendrix <i
     class="close material-icons">close</i></span>
    <span class="chip"><img src="images/img3.png"> Freddie Mercury <i
    class="close material-icons">close</i> </span>
</div>
```

Figure 5-17 depicts the output of the code.

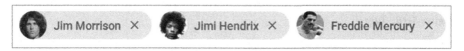

Figure 5-17. *Adding close buttons*

Materialize provides JavaScript functions to create chips. To use them, you need a target element where you wish to store all the created chips. See Listing 5-18.

Listing 5-18. A Target Element

```
<div class="row" style="margin-top: 10px;margin-left: 10px">
    <h1 class=" deep-orange-text darken-3">Materialize Training Session</h1>
    <h3>17/09/2016</h3>
    <div class="tags"></div>
</div>
<script type="text/javascript">
    $(function () {
        $('.tags').material_chip({
            data: [{
                tag: 'css',
            }, {
                tag: 'framework',
            }, {
                tag: 'javascript',
            },{
                tag: 'material design',
            }]
        });
    })
</script>
```

In Listing 5-18, you create a `<div>` tag and assign the tags class to it. The tags are associated with the page (about the Materialize training session, in your example). You use the material_chip function provided by Materialize to create chips using JavaScript. You pass the data to this function using the data property, which in turn contains a list of tags that should be displayed.

The output of the code is depicted in Figure 5-18.

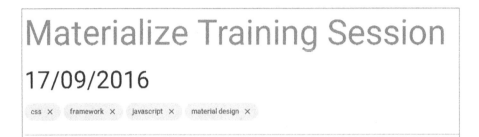

Figure 5-18. *Tags*

In the following sections, you will look into options that this function can accept and the format of the data.

The data provided to the `material_chip` function can contain three parameters:

- Tag: The content of the chip

- Image: The path of the image in order to include the image inside the chip

- Id: To assign an unique id to the chip

Listing 5-19 shows the typical structure of a single chip.

Listing 5-19. Typical Chip Structure

```
{
            tag: 'css',
            image:'images/img1.jpg',
            id:10
      }
```

The chip plug-in provides the options for customizing the experience with chips:

- data: Initialize Material's chip plug-in with an initial set of data.

- placeholder: The placeholder text that appears if there are chips present after initialization.

- secondaryPlaceHolder: The placeholder text that will appear if no chips are present after initialization.

To demonstrate the customization options, see Listing 5-20.

Listing 5-20. Chip Customization

```
<div class="row" style="margin-top: 10px;margin-left: 10px">
    <h1 class=" deep-orange-text darken-3">Materialize Training Session</h1>
    <h3>17/09/2016</h3>
    <div class="tags"></div>
</div>
<script type="text/javascript">
    $(function () {
        $('.tags').material_chip({
            data: [{
                tag: 'css',
            }, {
                tag: 'framework',
            }, {
                tag: 'javascript',
            },{
                tag: 'material design',
            }],
            secondaryPlaceholder:"No chips added. :(",
            placeholder:"Add more chips?"
        });
    })
</script>
```

In Listing 5-20, you initialize the material_chip function with the initial data set containing four tags and text for the default placeholder and secondary placeholder. Initializing chips using JavaScript also provides the option to add and remove chips. See Figure 5-19 for the results.

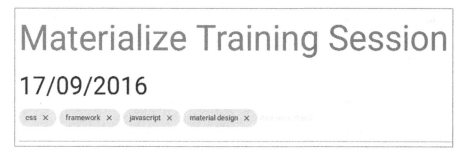

Figure 5-19. *Chip customication*

In Figure 5-19, you can see the Add more chips icon next to the material design chip as defined in the code. If you click the close icon on the css, framework, javascript, and material design chips, the *No chips added* text can be seen as defined in the code when no chips are present; see Figure 5-20.

Materialize Training Session
17/09/2016

Figure 5-20. *No chips added*

In the above code you initialize the material_chip function with initial data set consisting of four tags and text for default placeholder and secondary placeholder. Initializing chips using JavaScript also gives you the option to add and remove chips. The output of Listing 5-22 is shown in Figures 5-22 and 5-23, where one image shows the output when some chips are present and the other figure shows output when no chip are present.

Materialize's chip plug-in exposes events related to these chips which help keep track of which chip is selected, added, or removed. To demonstrate the events, take the preceding code and add the relevant code to it that will respond to chip events.

Materialize provides three events for the chips:

- chip.add: This event is triggered when a new chip is added.

- chip.delete: This event is triggered when a chip is removed.

- chip.select: This event is triggered when a user selects a chip by clicking on it.

Listing 5-21 contains an example of using the events.

Listing 5-21. Using Chip Events

```
<script type="text/javascript">
    $(function () {
        $('.tags').material_chip({
            data: [{
                tag: 'css',
            }, {
                tag: 'framework',
            }, {
                tag: 'javascript',
            },{
                tag: 'material design',
            }],
            secondaryPlaceholder:"No chips added. :(",
            placeholder:"Add more chips?"
        });
```

```
        //Add event handler
        $('.tags').on('chip.add', function(e, chip){
            alert("A chip was added");
        });

        $('.tags').on('chip.delete', function(e, chip){
            alert("A chip was removed")
        });

        $('.tags').on('chip.select', function(e, chip){
            alert("A chip was selected")
        });
    })
</script>
```

In Listing 5-21, you use jQuery's on method. An alert will be displayed whenever one of the events occurs. The message will specify which event occurred. In the code, you can see the chip.add, chip.delete, and chip.select functions.

The output of the code will result in the four chips being displayed.

If you try to remove the last chip (i.e. material design chip), you will receive a prompt stating that a chip has been removed as defined in the code.

Refer to Figure 5-21 to understand it better.

Figure 5-21. *A chip was removed*

Materialize also provides the facility to extract chip data when all the chips are present. For that, you call the material_chip function with a single parameter called data, as shown in the following line of code:

```
$('.tags').material_chip('data');
```

This returns an array of chip data.

Listing 5-22 shows an example of extracting chip data. You take the code from the preceding code example and use alerts to display the total number of chips on add and delete events.

Listing 5-22. Extracting Chip Data

```
<script type="text/javascript">
    $(function () {
        $('.tags').material_chip({
            data: [{
                tag: 'css',
            }, {
                tag: 'framework',
            }, {
                tag: 'javascript',
            },{
                tag: 'material design',
            }],
            secondaryPlaceholder:"No chips added. :(",
            placeholder:"Add more chips?"
        });
        //Add event handler
        $('.tags').on('chip.add', function(e, chip){
            var chipList = $('.tags').material_chip('data');
            alert("A chip was added. Total number of chips is: "+chipList.
            length);
        });

        $('.tags').on('chip.delete', function(e, chip){
            var chipList = $('.tags').material_chip('data');
            alert("A chip was Total number of chips is: "+chipList.length)
        });

        $('.tags').on('chip.select', function(e, chip){
            alert("A chip was selected")
        });
    })
</script>
```

In this code snippet, the chip data is stored using a variable called chipList. Since the data is in an array format, you use the length property to get the total count of the chips after the event has occurred. In this example, you add a new chip by typing the name of the chip, followed by pressing the Enter key. This will trigger the add event and show an alert with the updated count.

Similarly, if you remove a chip, it will display that a chip was removed and will state the total count is 3 because one chip was removed from the 4 chips, as depicted in Figure 5-22.

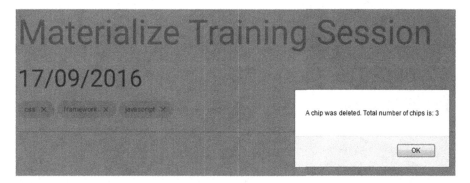

Figure 5-22. *A chip was deleted*

Collection

Materialize provides an innovative way of representing a list: the collection feature. When the list is represented using the collection property, each item appears in a container with a nice padding added around it, making it appear like rectangular blocks.

Listing 5-23 contains the code for the collection attribute.

Listing 5-23. The Collection Attribute

```
<div class="row" style="margin-top: 10px;margin-left: 10px">
    <div class="col m8">
    <h1 class=" deep-orange-text darken-3">Materialize Training Session</h1>
    <h3>17/09/2016</h3>
    <h4>Related topics</h4>
    <ul class="collection">
        <li class="collection-item">HTML</li>
        <li class="collection-item">CSS</li>
        <li class="collection-item">JS</li>
        <li class="collection-item">Material Design</li>
    </ul>
    </div>
</div>
```

In the preceding code, you create an unordered list that contains the name of the related topics. A list can be changed into a collection simply by adding a collection class to the <ul> tag and the collection-item to the individual list items. In the code, you have done just that by creating four topics: HTML, CSS, JS, and Material Design. Figure 5-23 shows the output.

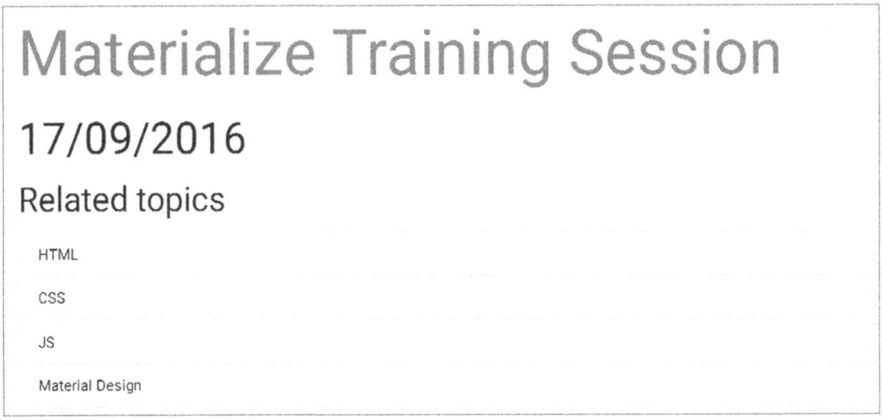

Materialize Training Session

17/09/2016

Related topics

HTML

CSS

JS

Material Design

Figure 5-23. *Four topics*

Instead of an unordered list, you can create a collection using anchors in `<div>` elements. Listing 5-24 contains the code snippet where you replace the `<li>` tags with anchor tags (`<a>`) and enclose them inside the `<div>` with the collection class.

Listing 5-24. A Colleciton with Anchors

```
<div class="row" style="margin-top: 10px;margin-left: 10px">
    <div class="col m8">
    <h1 class=" deep-orange-text darken-3">Materialize Training Session</h1>
    <h3>17/09/2016</h3>
    <h4>Related topics</h4>
    <div class="collection">
        <a href="!#" class="collection-item">HTML</a>
        <a href="!#" class="collection-item">CSS</a>
        <a href="!#" class="collection-item">JS</a>
        <a href="!#" class="collection-item active">Material Design</a>
    </div>
    </div>
</div>
```

Here you create a collection using anchors, as mentioned. You create four topics and you assign the active class to the last item in the collection (Material Design). The active anchor (Material Design) will be teal-colored due to the active class assigned to it, as depicted in Figure 5-24.

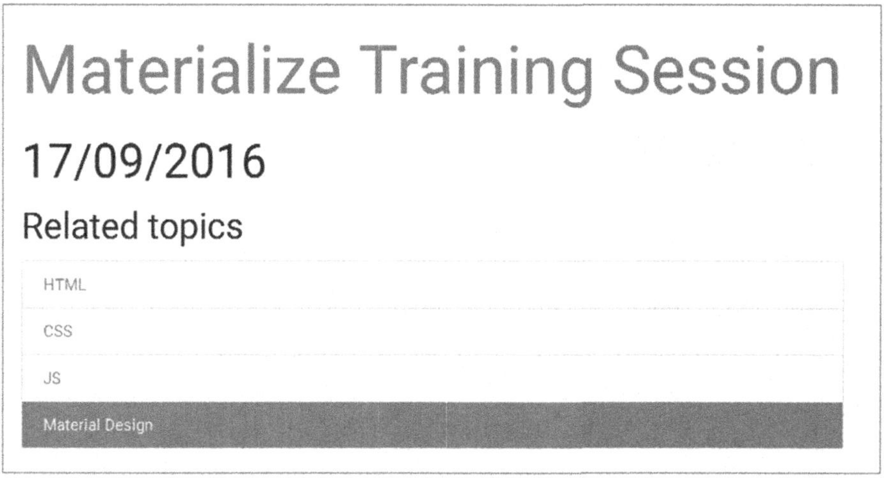

Figure 5-24. *Active class*

You can also enclose titles for the collection within the collection structure by simply placing the desired header inside the <div> with the collection class and assign the collection-header class to it. This indicates that the header is part of the collection structure. Then you need to add a with-header class to the parent <div>, which is defined by the collection class. Listing 5-25 shows the code.

Listing 5-25. Enclosing Titles

```
<div class="col m8">
    <h1 class=" deep-orange-text darken-3">Materialize Training Session</h1>
    <h3>17/09/2016</h3>
    <ul class="collection with-header">
        <li class="collection-header"><h4>Related topics</h4></li>
        <li class="collection-item">HTML</li>
        <li class="collection-item">CSS</li>
        <li class="collection-item">JS</li>
        <li class="collection-item">Material Design</li>
    </ul>
</div>
```

The output of this listing is shown in Figure 5-25.

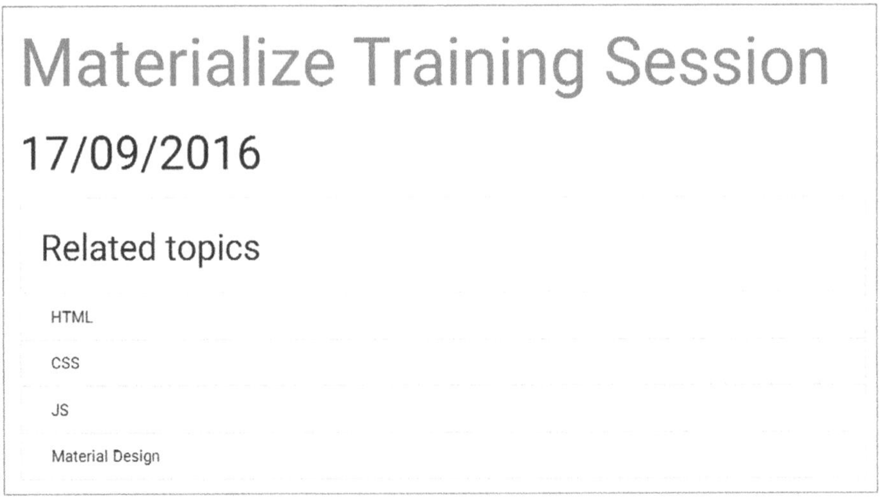

Materialize Training Session

17/09/2016

Related topics

HTML

CSS

JS

Material Design

Figure 5-25. *Enclosing titles*

At times, you may have to create a list with additional content such as badges and icons to make it more relevant and visually appealing. Suppose you want to show the number of people attending versus the number of people not attending the training sessions. You have two elements, Attending and Not Attending, with the numbers on the right side of the list item. You can actually add the content to the right side of the list items by adding a secondary-content class to it as depicted in Listing 5-26.

Listing 5-26. Adding Badges and Icons

```
<div class="col m8">
    <h1 class=" deep-orange-text darken-3">Materialize Training Session</h1>
    <h3>17/09/2016</h3>
    <ul class="collection with-header">
        <li class="collection-header"><h4>RSVP</h4></li>
        <li class="collection-item">Attending <span class="secondary-
        content">200</span> </li>
        <li class="collection-item">Not Attending <span class="secondary-
        content">50</span></li>
    </ul>
</div>
```

In Listing 5-26, you create a collection of two list items and assign a title to the collection. Then in the <li> tag, you add the secondary content in form of the <span> element with the secondary-content class to it. See Figure 5-26.

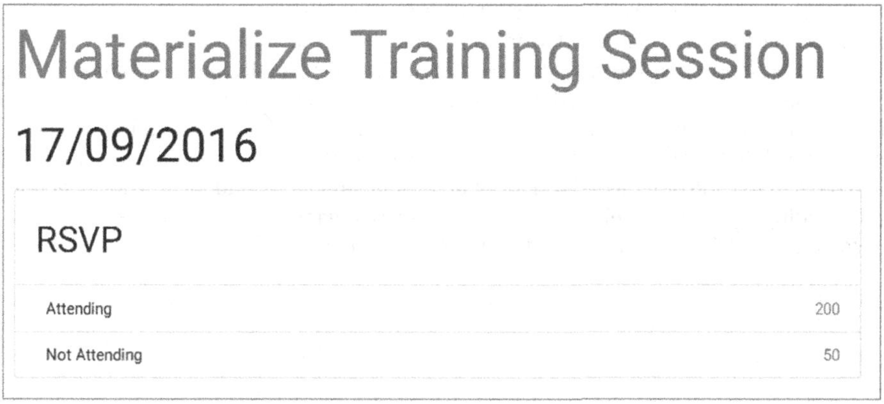

Materialize Training Session

17/09/2016

RSVP

Attending	200
Not Attending	50

Figure 5-26. *A collection of two list items*

You can also build a list similar to a contact list using the collection feature. You assign the avatar class, and use a name and contact information in a contact list. In the following example of event organizers, you use the code snippet shown in Listing 5-27.

Listing 5-27. Event Organizers

```
<div class="row" style="margin-top: 10px;margin-left: 10px">
    <div class="col m8">
    <h1 class=" deep-orange-text darken-3">Materialize Training Session</h1>
    <h3>17/09/2016</h3>
    <ul class="collection with-header">
        <li class="collection-header"><h4>Organizers</h4></li>
        <li class="collection-item avatar"><img src="images/img1.jpg"
        class="circle"/>
            <span class="title">Jim Morrison</span>
            <p>Event Organizer</p>
            <span class="secondary-content">JimMorrison@hoteleventabc.com</
            span>
        </li>
        <li class="collection-item avatar"><img src="images/img2.png"
        class="circle"/>
            <span class="title">Jimi Hendrix</span>
            <span class="secondary-content">JimiHendrix@concertevent77.com</
            span>
        </li>
    </ul>
    </div>
</div>
```

In Listing 5-27, you use the collection with the concept of an avatar. To create a collection with avatar, you need to add an avatar class to each <div> with the collection-item class. You can add the avatar to the collection by adding an image element as depicted in the preceding code. You use the circle class so that the image will fit properly in the collection area with rounded corners. You then add an inline <span> element with the title class that will be the title of the collection. In this example, you add the name of the organizers; you move on to add content beyond the title to collection by including a paragraph below as shown for the first organizer. You can also add the secondary-content class to add additional info. See Figure 5-27.

Figure 5-27. *Adding content*

To add to it, you can also incorporate a feature for the collection attribute that is touch enabled. The dismissible class is useful when you want to swipe the content from left to right to remove it from the list. It's typically handy while checking notifications when you want to remove the notification once it has been read.

Check the code bundle along with the book for the code on the dismissible feature.

Footer

A footer is an imperative component of a web page structure as it appears on the end of the page wherein it displays essential navigation information. It saves the user the time and effort by eliminating the need to scroll back to the top of the page to access core navigation. You can also include important information such as copyright and contact sections in the footer.

Take the preceding code for the organizers and add a footer to it, as shown in Listing 5-28.

Listing 5-28. Adding a Footer

```
<footer class="page-footer">
    <div class="container">
        <div class="row">
            <div class="col l6 s12">
                <h5 class="white-text">Materialize Training</h5>
                <p class="grey-text text-lighten-4">An introduction to
                framework by which you can leverage material design in your
                web application.</p>
            </div>
            <div class="col l4 offset-l2 s12">
                <h5 class="white-text">Links</h5>
                <ul>
                    <li><a class="grey-text text-lighten-3"
                    href="#!">Event</a></li>
                    <li><a class="grey-text text-lighten-3"
                    href="#!">Speakers</a></li>
                    <li><a class="grey-text text-lighten-3"
                    href="#!">Organizers</a></li>
                    <li><a class="grey-text text-lighten-3" href="#!">RSVP</
                    a></li>
                </ul>
            </div>
        </div>
    </div>
    <div class="footer-copyright">
        <div class="container">
            &copy; 2016 Copyright Materializecss
        </div>
    </div>
</footer>
```

In Listing 5-28, you use the <footer> tag and add the page-footer class. You then
create the container for the footer and define the content and links to be placed in the
footer by using simple HTML code. Finally, you create a <div> element to define the
footer-copyright class and design a container for the copyright information. Then you
wrap up the footer feature by using an </footer> tag.

Refer to the code bundle for the entire code. Figure 5-28 shows the output of the code
wherein you can scroll down for the footer section.

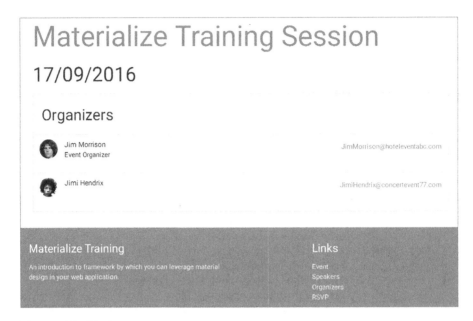

Figure 5-28. *The footer*

Forms

Forms are a useful resource to allow users to enter data and to enable this collected data to be sent to servers for processing purposes. Materialize's Forms components are versatile and easy to code. In Materialize, you can add transitions and smoothness to make it an immersive experience.

Input Field

Input fields are the most basic form element; they accept inputs from a user. In Materialize, you must wrap your input field and its associated label in a <div> element with the input-field class. By wrapping the elements this way, you can easily animate the labels using a bit of jQuery. This wrapping has to be performed for input fields and text areas only.

Listing 5-29 show the code snippet for creating the initial input fields in Forms.

Listing 5-29. Input Fields

```
<div class="container">
<div class="row" style="margin-top: 10px;margin-left: 10px">
    <h1 class=" deep-orange-text darken-3">Materialize Training Session</h1>
    <h3>17/09/2016</h3>
    <h5>Visitor registration</h5>
```

```
<div class="row">
    <div class="col m6 input-field">
    <label for="firstName">First Name</label>
        <input type="text" name="firstName" id="firstName"
        placeholder="Please enter a Firstname"/>
    </div>
    <div class="col m6 input-field">
        <label for="lastName">Last Name</label>
        <input type="text" name="lastName" id="lastName"
        placeholder="Please enter a Lastname"/>
    </div>
    </div>

</div>
</div>
```

In this code, you build a registration form for the training event. You start with adding input fields for the first and last name of the person. Since you need the fields next to each other, you place these fields in two <div>s, each having a col m6 class denoting that it will consume half the space of the total area. Next, you add the input-field class to them, thus creating a wrapper for your input fields and their associated labels. Then you add the necessary input fields to these <div>s. Figure 5-29 depicts the output of the code so far.

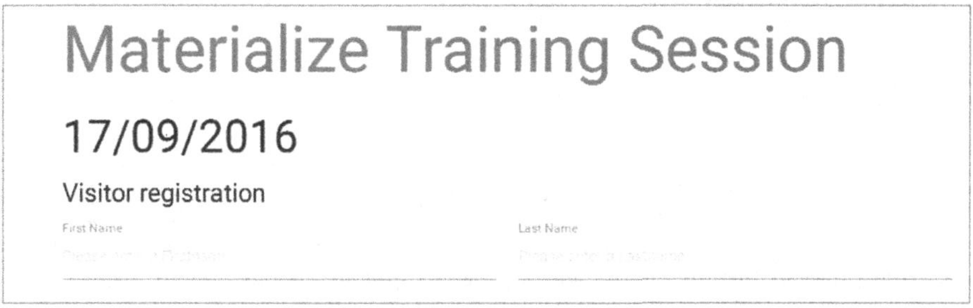

Figure 5-29. *Fields*

If there is no explicit placeholder, the label will act as a placeholder. If you specify the placeholder, then it will reflect in the field, as depicted in Listing 5-30.

Listing 5-30. A Placeholder

```
<div class="container">
<div class="row" style="margin-top: 10px;margin-left: 10px">
    <h1 class=" deep-orange-text darken-3">Materialize Training Session</h1>
    <h3>17/09/2016</h3>
    <h5>Visitor registration</h5>
        <div class="row">
```

```
                <div class="col m6 input-field">
                <label for="firstName">First Name</label>
                    <input type="text" name="firstName" id="firstName"
                    placeholder="Enter First Name"/>
                </div>
                <div class="col m6 input-field">
                    <label for="lastName">Last Name</label>
                    <input type="text" name="lastName" id="lastName"
                    placeholder="Enter Last Name"/>
                </div>
                </div>

        </div>
        </div>
```

In this code, you add the Enter First Name and Enter Last Name placeholders, which will result in the output in Figure 5-30.

Figure 5-30. *Placeholders in action*

Materialize makes the best use of HTML5 validation and displays properly validated or erroneous fields with green and red validation states, respectively. You need to add a `validate` class to the target input field. Create an input field of type "email" which supports HTML5 validation. You will show the validation effect when a valid or invalid value has been entered. See Listing 5-31 for the code.

Listing 5-31. *Vaildation*

```
<div class="container">
<div class="row" style="margin-top: 10px;margin-left: 10px">
    <h1 class=" deep-orange-text darken-3">Materialize Training Session</h1>
    <h3>17/09/2016</h3>
    <h5>Visitor registration</h5>
        <div class="row">
            <div class="col m6 input-field">
            <label for="firstName">First Name</label>
```

```
            <input type="text" name="firstName" id="firstName"
            placeholder="Please enter a Firstname"/>
        </div>
        <div class="col m6 input-field">
            <label for="lastName">First Name</label>
            <input type="text" name="lastName" id="lastName"
            placeholder="Please enter a Firstname"/>
        </div>
        </div>
        <div class="row">
            <div class="input-field col m12">
                <input id="email" type="email" class="validate">
                <label for="email">Email</label>
            </div>
        </div>
    </div>
</div>
</div>
```

Figure 5-31 depicts the green line below the Email field when you enter a valid email address.

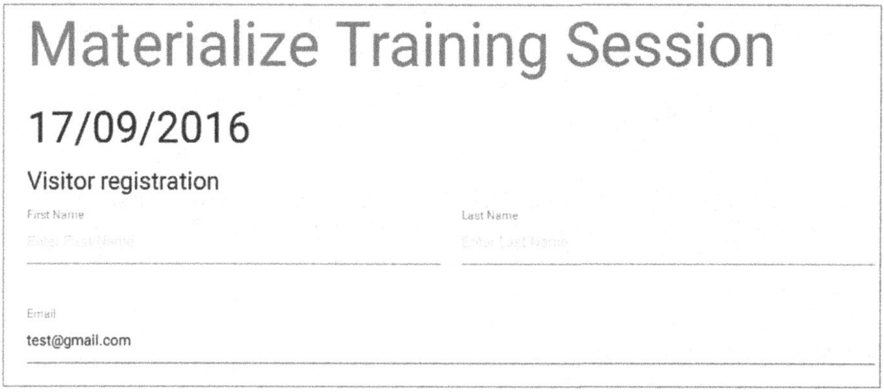

Figure 5-31. *Valid email address*

Figure 5-32 depicts the red line which indicates that there is an invalid email address.

Materialize Training Session

17/09/2016

Visitor registration

First Name   Last Name

Email

material,magazine,raven

Figure 5-32. *Invalid email address*

You can add an icon before the email field by using the code in Listing 5-32.

Listing 5-32. Adding the Icon

```
<div class="row">
                <div class="input-field col m12">
                                <i class="material-icons prefix">email</i>
                    <input id="email" type="email" class="validate">
                    <label for="email">Email</label>
                </div>
                </div>
```

Validation in HTML5 is well ingrained by showing fields in error or valid states. You can further add custom messages that will be shown in case of an error or successful validation. Listing 5-33 depicts the use of data-error and data-success attributes to add messages for the label.

Listing 5-33. Adding Messages

```
<div class="row">
            <div class="input-field col m12">
                <i class="material-icons prefix">email</i>
                <input id="email" type="email" class="validate">
                <label for="email" data-error="invalid email address" data-
                success="Thank you!">Email</label>
            </div>
        </div>
```

The output of the code will show the message if you do not enter the valid email type. At the same time, you can also see the Email icon next to the Email field, as depicted in Figure 5-33.

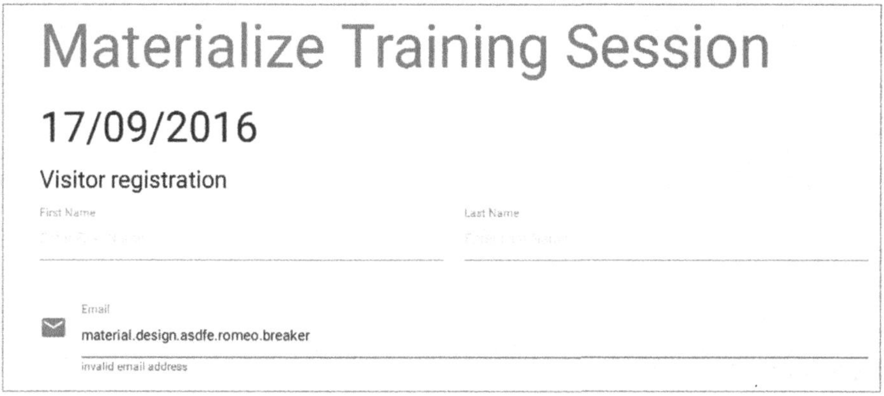

Figure 5-33. *Icons*

Textarea

Textarea is similar to the input field. You need to create a textarea element followed by adding the materialize-textarea class. Listing 5-34 shows the code snippet.

Listing 5-34. Textarea

```
<div class="row">
        <div class="input-field col m12">
            <textarea id="message" class="message materialize-textarea"
            name="message"></textarea>
            <label for="message">Message</label>
        </div>
    </div>
```

The output of the code will result in a text area for the Message field, as depicted in Figure 5-34.

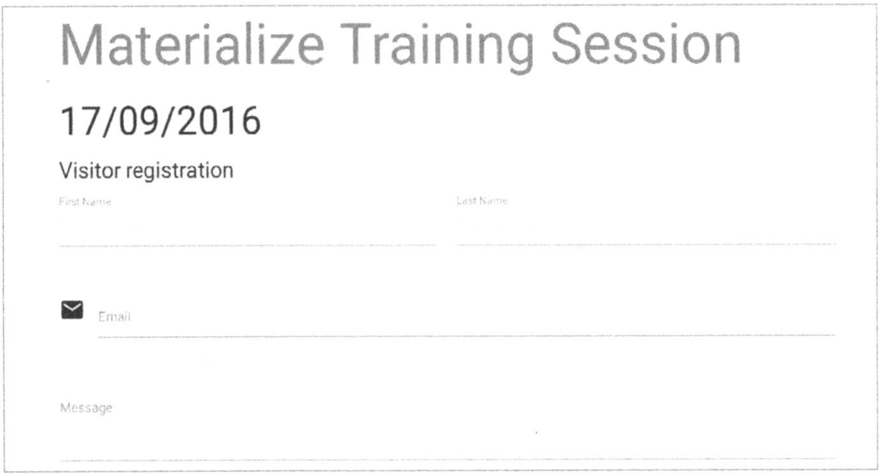

Materialize Training Session

17/09/2016

Visitor registration

First Name   Last Name

✉ Email

Message

Figure 5-34. *Textarea*

Select

The Select feature allows the user to select from multiple options. To create a simple select element, create a select with some options in it. Enclose it into the input-field. Then initialize the select element using JavaScript. By default, the select allows selection of single option. You can change this to multiple select options by simply adding an attribute named `multiple` to the `select` property. You also create another select element that asks about technology awareness.

The entire code snippet is shown in in Listing 5-35.

Listing 5-35. The Select Feature

```
<div class="container">
    <div class="row" style="margin-top: 10px;margin-left: 10px">
        <h1 class=" deep-orange-text darken-3">Materialize Training
        Session</h1>
        <h3>17/09/2016</h3>
        <h5>Visitor registration</h5>
        <div class="row">
            <div class="col m6 input-field">
                <label for="firstName">First Name</label>
                <input type="text" name="firstName" id="firstName"
                placeholder="Enter a Firstname"/>
            </div>
            <div class="col m6 input-field">
                <label for="lastName">Last Name</label>
                <input type="text" name="lastName" id="lastName"
                placeholder="Enter a Lastname"/>
            </div>
```

```html
        </div>
        <div class="row">
            <div class="input-field col m6">
                <input id="email" type="email" class="validate">
                <label for="email" data-error="invalid email address" data-
                success="Thank you!">Email</label>
            </div>
            <div class="input-field col s6">
                <select id="gender">
                    <option value="" disabled selected>Choose an option</
                    option>
                    <option value="male">Male</option>
                    <option value="female">Female</option>
                </select>
                <label>Gender</label>
            </div>
        </div>
        <div class="row">
            <div class="input-field col s12">
                <select id="techaware" multiple>
                    <option value="" disabled selected>Choose an option</
                    option>
                    <option value="html">HTML</option>
                    <option value="css">CSS</option>
                    <option value="js">JavaScript</option>
                    <option value="jquery">jQuery</option>
                    <option value="android">Android</option>
                </select>
                <label>Technology awareness</label>
            </div>
        </div>
        <div class="row">
            <div class="input-field col m12">
                <textarea id="message" class="message materialize-textarea"
                name="message"></textarea>
                <label for="message">Message</label>
            </div>
        </div>
    </div>
</div>
<script type="text/javascript">
    $(document).ready(function() {
        $('select').material_select();
    });
</script>
```

In this code, you create two options: Male and Female for the Gender field. Next, you created a Technology Awareness field to see the multiple options. You initialize the `select` function on all select elements to give it an appropriate look and feel. The function must be initialized compulsorily for the select functionality to work correctly. If you click the Technology Awareness field, you can see the multiple options in Figure 5-35.

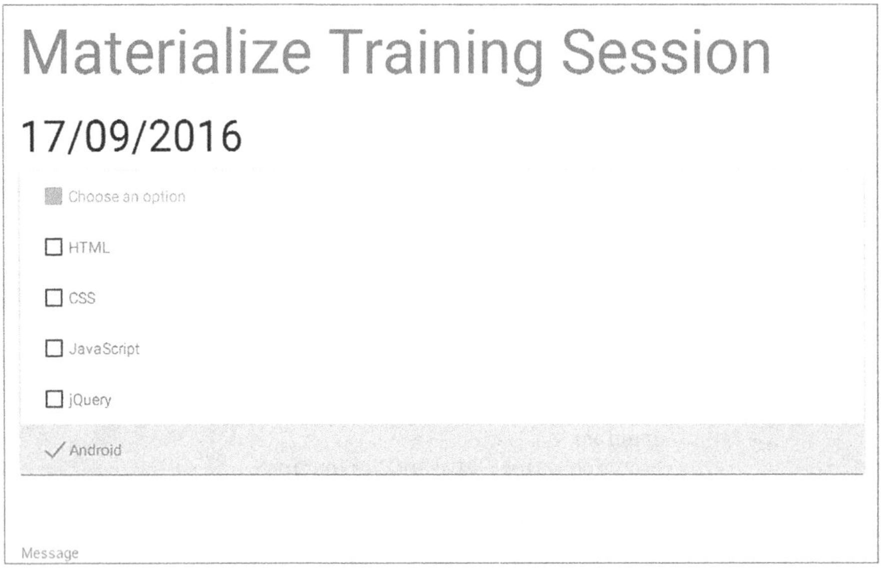

Materialize Training Session
17/09/2016

- Choose an option
- ☐ HTML
- ☐ CSS
- ☐ JavaScript
- ☐ jQuery
- ✓ Android

Message

Figure 5-35. Many options

Images can be added to the options within the select element using the `data-icon` attribute; see Listing 5-36.

Listing 5-36. Adding Images

```
<div class="input-field col s6">
            <select id="invitationby">
                <option value="" disabled selected>Choose an option</
                option>
                <option value="html" data-icon="images/img1.jpg"
                class="circle">Jim Morrison</option>
                <option value="css" data-icon="images/img2.png"
                class="circle">Jimi Hendrix</option>
            </select>
            <label>Invited By</label>
        </div>
```

In Listing 5-36, you create an input field with the *Invited by* text. Next, you create a select with three options. First you add the `disabled` class to the first option, which is actually accompanied by the text "Choose an option". Remember that *Choose an option* is just for informing the user to select the following two options, which you are going to define next. Hence, you have added a `disabled` class to the *Choose an option* text.

You add two images and the `circle` class to the next two options, for Jim Morrison and Jimi Hendrix.

Figure 5-36 depicts the output of the code when you click on the Choose an Option input field in the Invited By field.

Figure 5-36. *Choosing an option*

Radio

Radio selections are applicable when users have to select only one of the options from the provided list. To demonstrate this, you add an Additional Members text under which you define the various radio options; see Listing 5-37.

Listing 5-37. Radio Buttons

```
<div class="row">
        <h5>Additional members</h5>
        <p>
            <input name="members" type="radio" id="one" />
            <label for="one">+1 member</label>
        </p>
        <p>
            <input name="members" type="radio" id="two" />
            <label for="two">+2 member</label>
        </p>
        <p>
            <input name="members" type="radio" id="three"  />
            <label for="three">+3 members</label>
        </p>
        <p>
```

```
                <input name="members" type="radio" id="many"
                disabled="disabled" />
                <label for="many">More than 4</label>
        </p>
    </div>
```

In this code, you create a set of radio buttons that are assigned the *members* input name followed by the *radio* type. You deactivate the final radio option (More than 4) by assigning the disabled class to it.

Figure 5-37 depicts the radio buttons where you can select only one option (with the last option disabled). The +3 members option has been clicked to demonstrate that only one option can be selected at a time.

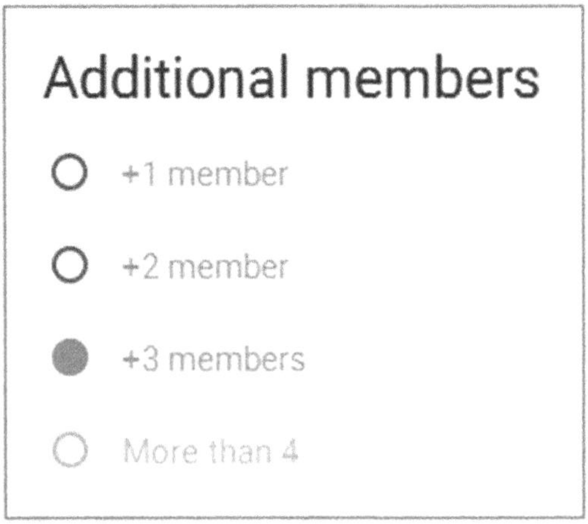

Figure 5-37. Radio buttons

Checkboxes

Checkboxes are used to answer various options in a Yes or No format. In Listing 5-38, you add a section called Terms and Conditions in the same form where you need to accept the terms and conditions to proceed.

Listing 5-38. Adding a Section

```
<div class="row">
        <p>
                <input type="checkbox" id="acceptTC" />
                <label for="acceptTC">Accept Terms and Conditions</label>
        </p>
    </div>
```

You have assigned the checkbox type to the input and used an id which is assigned to the for attribute for the label with the Accept Terms and Conditions text.

When you execute the code, you will see a checkbox with the Accept Terms and Conditions text. Upon clicking the checkbox, the output will show the checked sign.

Refer to Figure 5-38 to see the output when the code is executed and later when it is checked.

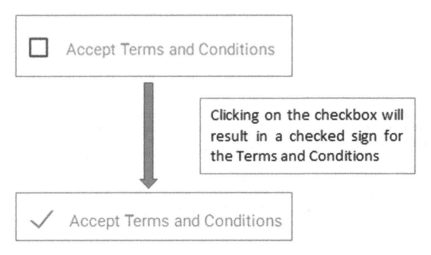

Figure 5-38. *Checkboxes*

Switches

Switches are a variant of the checkboxes with better aesthetics and feel. To create an immersive experience, it is a handy alternative to the checkbox. These switches look like real-world switches and are common in Android and IOS systems.

Listing 5-39 shows an example of the switches functionality.

Listing 5-39. Switches

```
<div class="row">
          <p class="col m3">Accept Terms and Conditions</p>
          <div class="col m3">
          <div class="switch" style="margin: 15px 0;">
              <label>
                  No
                  <input type="checkbox" id="acceptTC">
                  <span class="lever"></span>
                  Yes
              </label>
          </div>
      </div>
   </div>
```

127

In Listing 5-39, you replace the checkbox with a switch. You create a <div> with the class switch and use the input type within it as checkbox and introduce an inline <span> element with the lever class assigned to it. See Figure 5-39.

Figure 5-39. *A switch*

DatePicker

A DatePicker is a very common component in forms. In Materialize you can create a DatePicker wherein the user can easily fill in the specific date without worrying about the format. See Listing 5-40.

Listing 5-40. DatePicker

```
<div class="col m6">
                <label for="dob">Date of Birth</label>
                <input type="date" class="dob" id="dob" placeholder="Enter
                Date of Birth">
            </div>
```

In Listing 5-40, you create a <div> and create a label. Then you define the input type and assign the date type to it and assign a class dob to it. Incidentally, the value of the class is the value of the label's for attribute. You enter a placeholder for the same. Then you initialize the JavaScript for Materialize to bind the DatePicker functionality to this new field.

Listing 5-41 shows the code for the JavaScript functionality.

Listing 5-41. JavaScript

```
$('.dob').pickadate({
      selectMonths: true,
      selectYears: 35
   });
```

In Listing 5-41, you initialize the DatePicker with two options: one that allows the user to choose the month or the other which states the years from the past. In your example, you have set the same to 35.

Figure 5-40 depicts the output of the code when you click on the *Date of Birth* field.

Figure 5-40. *DatePicker*

Summary

In this chapter, you looked at several components such as badges, buttons, cards, chips, and forms to name a few. You looked at how the badges can be used to visually indicate the updates in the count. Further, you looked at the buttons and various customizations associated with it. Next, you saw how we utilized components such as cards and chips along with their implementation like you would use in a real-time scenario in Android Phones and tablets. Finally, we wound up with forms and utilities such as DatePicker and Switches which enhance the way forms are used actually.

After going through all the chapters in this book, you most likely have come to grips with the concepts in Materialize at an introductory level and will want to delve deep into the framework to utilize it in your web projects or pursue it further to create interactive websites.

Material Design helps impart continuity, and enables a powerful and consistent experience across your websites. It helps create uniformity in a concise way without much ambiguity. With responsiveness baked in, it enhances the user experience to a large extent. Natural motions, animations, and transitions are streamlined significantly to create a responsive, immersive experience. With HTML, CSS, and JavaScript as its building blocks, it helps designers get started in seconds and match good design in an innovative manner.

For our readers, we have created a sample product page for Apple iPhone 6 to illustrate how simple it is to create webpages using this powerful framework. Go to `http://www.apress.com/us/book/9781484223482` to download the bonus chapter and all accompanying source code.

As with everything, the learning curve is really steep in Materialize and with the web evolving faster than expected, there will be additions and updates to this awesome framework. Still, with its effective methodologies, Materialize is the go-to framework to create Material Design-based intuitive websites for a seamless user experience.

Index

■ W, X, Y, Z

Get the eBook for only $4.99!

Why limit yourself?

Now you can take the weightless companion with you wherever you go and access your content on your PC, phone, tablet, or reader.

Since you've purchased this print book, we are happy to offer you the eBook for just $4.99.

Convenient and fully searchable, the PDF version enables you to easily find and copy code—or perform examples by quickly toggling between instructions and applications.

To learn more, go to http://www.apress.com/us/shop/companion or contact support@apress.com.

All Apress eBooks are subject to copyright. All rights are reserved by the Publisher, whether the whole or part of the material is concerned, specifically the rights of translation, reprinting, reuse of illustrations, recitation, broadcasting, reproduction on microfilms or in any other physical way, and transmission or information storage and retrieval, electronic adaptation, computer software, or by similar or dissimilar methodology now known or hereafter developed. Exempted from this legal reservation are brief excerpts in connection with reviews or scholarly analysis or material supplied specifically for the purpose of being entered and executed on a computer system, for exclusive use by the purchaser of the work. Duplication of this publication or parts thereof is permitted only under the provisions of the Copyright Law of the Publisher's location, in its current version, and permission for use must always be obtained from Springer. Permissions for use may be obtained through RightsLink at the Copyright Clearance Center. Violations are liable to prosecution under the respective Copyright Law.

Printed in the United States
By Bookmasters